John V Fleming

BUREAUCRACY

BY LUDWIG VON MISES

NEW HAVEN
YALE UNIVERSITY PRESS
1944

PREFACE

THE main issue in present-day social and political conflicts is whether or not man should give away freedom, private initiative, and individual responsibility and surrender to the guardianship of a gigantic apparatus of compulsion and coercion, the socialist state. Should authoritarian totalitarianism be substituted for individualism and democracy? Should the citizen be transformed into a *subject*, a subordinate in an all-embracing army of conscripted labor, bound to obey unconditionally the orders of his superiors? Should he be deprived of his most precious privilege to choose means and ends and to shape his own life?

Our age has witnessed a triumphal advance of the socialist cause. As much as half a century ago an eminent British statesman, Sir William Harcourt, asserted: "We are all socialists now." [1] At that time this statement was premature as far as Great Britain was concerned, but today it is almost literally true for that country, once the cradle of modern liberty. It is no less true with regard to continental Europe. America alone is still free to choose. And the decision of the American people will determine the outcome for the whole of mankind.

The problems involved in the antagonism between socialism and capitalism can be attacked from various viewpoints. At present it seems as if an investigation of the expansion of bureaucratic agencies is the most expedient avenue of approach. An analysis of bureaucratism offers an excellent opportunity to recognize the fundamental problems of the controversy.

Although the evolution of bureaucratism has been very

1. Cf. G. M. Trevelyan, *A Shortened History of England* (London, 1942), p. 510.

rapid in these last years, America is still, compared with the rest of the world, only superficially afflicted. It shows only a few of the characteristic features of bureaucratic management. A scrutiny of bureaucratism in this country would be incomplete therefore if it did not deal with some aspects and results of the movement which became visible only in countries with an older bureaucratic tradition. Such a study must analyze the experiences of the classical countries of bureaucratism—France, Germany, and Russia.

However it is not the object of such occasional references to European conditions to obscure the radical difference which exists, with regard to bureaucratism, between the political and social mentality of America and that of continental Europe. To the American mind the notion of an *Obrigkeit*, a government the authority of which is not derived from the people, was and is unknown. It is even extremely difficult to explain to a man for whom the writings of Milton and Paine, the Declaration of Independence, the Constitution and the Gettysburg Address are the fountain springs of political education, what this German term *Obrigkeit* implies and what an *Obrigkeits-Staat* is. Perhaps the two following quotations will help to elucidate the matter.

On January 15, 1838, the Prussian Minister of the Interior, G. A. R. von Rochow, declared in reply to a petition of citizens of a Prussian city: "It is not seemly for a subject to apply the yardstick of his wretched intellect to the acts of the Chief of the State and to arrogate to himself, in haughty insolence, a public judgment about their fairness." This was in the days in which German liberalism challenged absolutism, and public opinion vehemently resented this piece of overbearing bureaucratic pretension.

Half a century later German liberalism was stone dead. The Kaiser's *Sozialpolitik*, the statist system of government interference with business and of aggressive nationalism, had supplanted it. Nobody minded when the Rector of the Imperial University of Strassburg quietly characterized the German system of government thus: "Our officials . . . will never tolerate anybody's wresting the power from their hands, certainly not parliamentary majorities whom we know how to deal with in a masterly way. No kind of rule is endured so easily or accepted so gratefully as that of high-minded and highly educated civil servants. The German State is a State of the supremacy of officialdom—let us hope that it will remain so." [2]

Such aphorisms could not be enunciated by any American. It could not happen here.

2. Georg Friedrich Knapp in his Presidential Address, delivered on May 1, 1891. This speech was published in many reprints. The words quoted are to be found on p. 86 of the 1909 edition of *Die Landarbeiter in Knechtschaft und Freiheit.*

CONTENTS

BUREAUCRACY

INTRODUCTION

I. THE OPPROBRIOUS CONNOTATION OF THE TERM BU-REAUCRACY

THE terms *bureaucrat, bureaucratic,* and *bureaucracy* are clearly invectives. Nobody calls himself a bureaucrat or his own methods of management bureaucratic. These words are always applied with an opprobrious connotation. They always imply a disparaging criticism of persons, institutions, or procedures. Nobody doubts that bureaucracy is thoroughly bad and that it should not exist in a perfect world.

The abusive implication of the terms in question is not limited to America and other democratic countries. It is a universal phenomenon. Even in Prussia, the paragon of authoritarian government, nobody wanted to be called a bureaucrat. The Prussian king's *wirklicher geheimer Ober-Regierungsrat* was proud of his dignity and of the power that it bestowed. His conceit delighted in the reverence of his subordinates and of the populace. He was imbued with the idea of his own importance and infallibility. But he would have deemed it an impudent insult if somebody had the effrontery to call him a bureaucrat. He was, in his own opinion, not a bureaucrat but a civil servant, his Majesty's mandatory, a functionary of the State unswervingly attending day and night to the welfare of the nation.

It is noteworthy that the "progressives" whom the critics of bureaucracy make responsible for its spread do not venture to defend the bureaucratic system. On the contrary, they join those whom they in other respects scorn as "reactionaries" in condemning it. For, they maintain, these bureaucratic methods are not at all essential for the utopia at which they themselves are aiming. Bureaucracy, they say, is rather the unsatisfactory way in which the capitalist system tries to come to an arrangement with the inexorable trend toward its own disappearance. The inevitable final triumph of socialism will abolish not only capitalism but bureaucratism also. In the happy world of tomorrow, in the blessed paradise of all-round planning, there will no longer be any bureaucrats. The common man will be paramount; the people themselves will take care of all their affairs. Only narrow-minded bourgeois can fall prey to the error that bureaucracy gives a foretaste of what socialism has in store for mankind.

Thus everyone seems to agree that bureaucracy is an evil. But it is no less true that nobody has ever tried to determine in unambiguous language what bureaucracy really means. The word is generally used loosely. Most people would be embarrassed if somebody were to ask them for a precise definition and explanation. How can they condemn bureaucracy and bureaucrats if they do not even know what the terms mean?

2. THE AMERICAN CITIZEN'S INDICTMENT OF BUREAUCRATISM

An American, asked to specify his complaints about the evils of progressing bureaucratization, might say something like this:

"Our traditional American system of government was based on the separation of the legislative, the executive, and the judicial powers and on a fair division of jurisdiction between the Union and the States. The legislators, the most important executives, and many of the judges were chosen by election. Thus the people, the voters, were supreme. Moreover, none of the three arms of the government had the right to interfere with the private affairs of the citizens. The law-abiding citizen was a free man.

"But now, for many years and especially since the appearance of the New Deal, powerful forces are on the point of substituting for this old and well-tried democratic system the tyrannical rule of an irresponsible and arbitrary bureaucracy. The bureaucrat does not come into office by election of the voters but by appointment of another bureaucrat. He has arrogated a good deal of the legislative power. Government commissions and bureaus issue decrees and regulations undertaking the management and direction of every aspect of the citizens' lives. Not only do they regulate matters which hitherto have been left to the discretion of the individual; they do not shrink from decreeing what is virtually a repeal of duly enacted laws. By means of this quasi-legislation the bureaus usurp the power to decide many important matters according to their own judgment of the merits of each case, that is, quite arbitrarily. The rulings and judgments of the bureaus are enforced by Federal officials. The purported judicial review is in fact illusory. Every day the bureaucrats assume more power; pretty soon they will run the whole country.

"There cannot be any doubt that this bureaucratic system is essentially antiliberal, undemocratic, and un-American, that it is contrary to the spirit and to the letter of the Constitution, and that it is a replica of the totalitarian methods of Stalin and Hitler. It is imbued with a fanatical hostility to free enterprise and private property. It paralyzes the conduct of business and lowers the productivity of labor. By heedless spending it squanders the nation's wealth. It is inefficient and wasteful. Although it styles what it does planning, it has no definite plans and aims. It lacks unity and uniformity; the various bureaus and agencies work at cross-purposes. The outcome is a disintegration of the whole social apparatus of production and distribution. Poverty and distress are bound to follow."

This vehement indictment of bureaucracy is, by and large, an adequate although emotional description of present-day trends in American government. But it misses the point as it makes bureaucracy and the bureaucrats responsible for an evolution the causes of which must be sought for elsewhere. Bureaucracy is but a consequence and a symptom of things and changes much more deeply rooted.

The characteristic feature of present-day policies is the trend toward a substitution of government control for free enterprise. Powerful political parties and pressure groups are fervently asking for public control of all economic activities, for thorough government planning, and for the nationalization of business. They aim at full government control of education and at the socialization of the medical profession. There is no sphere of human activity that they would not be prepared to subordinate to regimentation by the authorities. In their eyes, state control is the panacea for all ills.

These enthusiastic advocates of government omnipotence are very modest in the appraisal of the role they themselves play in the evolution toward totalitarianism. The trend toward socialism, they contend, is inevitable. It is the necessary and unavoidable tendency of historical evolution. With Karl Marx they maintain that socialism is bound to come "with the inexorability of a law of nature." Private ownership of the means of production, free enterprise, capitalism, the profit system are doomed. The "wave of the future" carries men toward the earthly paradise of full government control. The champions of totalitarianism call themselves "progressives" precisely because they pretend to have comprehended the meaning of the portents. And they ridicule and disparage as "reactionaries" all those who try to resist the working of forces which—as they say—no human effort is strong enough to stop.

Because of these "progressive" policies new offices and government agencies thrive like mushrooms. The bureaucrats multiply and are anxious to restrict, step by step, the individual citizen's freedom to act. Many citizens, i.e., those whom the "progressives" scorn as "reactionaries," resent this encroachment upon their affairs, and blame the incompetence and wastefulness of the bureaucrats. But these opponents have hitherto been only a minority. The proof is that, in the past elections, they were not in a position to poll a majority of the votes. The "progressives," the adamant foes of free enterprise and private initiative and fanatical champions of totalitarian government control of business, defeated them.

It is a fact that the policy of the New Deal has been supported by the voters. Nor is there any doubt that this policy will be entirely abandoned if the voters withdraw their favor from it. The United States is still a democracy. The Constitution is still intact. Elections are still free. The voters do not cast their ballot under duress. It is therefore not correct to say that the bureaucratic system carried its victory by unconstitutional and undemocratic methods. The lawyers may be right in questioning the legality of some minor points. But as a whole the New Deal was backed by Congress. Congress made the laws and appropriated the money.

Of course, America is faced with a phenomenon that the framers of the Constitution did not foresee and could not foresee: the voluntary abandonment of congressional rights. Congress has in many instances surrendered the function of legislation to government agencies and commissions, and it has relaxed its budgetary control through the allocation of large appropriations for expenditures, which the Administration has to determine in detail. The right of Congress to delegate some of its powers temporarily is not uncontested. In the case of the National Recovery Administration the Supreme Court declared it unconstitutional. But delegations of power formulated in a more cautious way are an almost regular practice. At any rate, Congress, in acting this way, has *hitherto* not been at variance with the declared will of the majority of the sovereign people.

On the other hand, we must realize that delegation of power is the main instrument of modern dictatorship. It is by virtue of delegation of power that Hitler and his Cabinet rule Germany. It is by delegation of power that the British Left wants to establish its dictatorship and to transform Great Britain into a socialist commonwealth. It is obvious that delegation of power can be used as a quasi-constitutional disguise for a dictatorship. But this is certainly not the case at present in this country. Congress has undoubtedly still the legal right and the actual might to take back all the power it has delegated. The voters still have the right and the power to return senators and representatives who are radically opposed to any abandonment of congressional powers. In the United States bureaucracy is based on constitutional grounds.

Nor is it correct to deem as unconstitutional the progressing concentration of jurisdictional powers in the central government and the resulting diminution of the importance of the States. Washington has not openly usurped any constitutional powers of the States. The equilibrium in the distribution of powers between the Federal Government and the States as established by the Constitution has been seriously disturbed because the new powers that the authorities acquired for the most part accrued to the Union and not to the States. This is not the effect of sinister machinations on the part of mysterious Washington cliques, eager to curb the States and to establish centralization. It is the consequence of the fact that the United States is an economic unit with a uniform monetary and credit system and with free mobility of commodities, capital, and men among the States. In such a country government control of business must be centralized. It would be out of the question to leave it to the individual States. If each State were free to control business according to its own plans, the unity of the domestic market would disintegrate. State control of business would be practicable only if every State were in a position to separate its territory from the rest of the nation by trade and migration barriers and an autonomous monetary and credit policy. As nobody seriously suggests breaking up the economic unity of the nation, it has been necessary to entrust the control of business to the Union. It is in the nature of a system of government control of business to aim at the utmost centralization. The autonomy of the States as guaranteed by the Constitution is realizable only under a system of free enterprise. In voting for government control of business the voters implicitly, although unwittingly, are voting for more centralization.

Those who criticize bureaucracy make the mistake of directing their attacks against a symptom only and not against the seat of the evil. It makes no difference whether the innumerable decrees regimenting every aspect of the citizen's economic activities are issued directly by a law, duly passed by Congress, or by a commission or government agency to which power has been given by a law and by the allocation of money. What people are really complaining about is the fact that the government has embarked upon such totalitarian policies, not the technical procedures applied in their establishment. It would make little difference if Congress had not endowed these agencies with quasi-legislative functions and had reserved to itself the right to issue all decrees required for the conduct of their functions.

Once price control is declared a task of government, an indefinite number of price ceilings must be fixed and many of them must, with changing conditions, be altered again and again. This power is vested in the Office of Price Administration. But the sway of its bureaucrats would not be impaired *substantially* if they were under the necessity of approaching Congress for legislating such ceilings. Congress would be flooded by a multitude of bills the content of which would extend beyond the range of its competence. The members of Congress would lack both the time and the information to examine seriously the proposals elaborated by the various subdivisions of the OPA. No choice would be left to them other than trusting the chief of the office and its employees and voting en bloc for the bills or repealing the law giving the Administration the power to control prices. It would be out of the question for the members of Congress to look into the matter with the same conscientiousness and scrupulousness they ordinarily apply in deliberating about policies and laws.

Parliamentary procedures are an adequate method for dealing with the framing of laws needed by a community based on private ownership of the means of production, free enterprise, and consumers' sovereignty. They are essentially inappropriate for the conduct of affairs under government omnipotence. The makers of the Constitution never dreamed of a system of government under which the authorities would have to determine the prices of pepper and of oranges, of photographic cameras and of razor blades, of neckties and of paper napkins. But if such a contingency had occurred to them, they surely would have considered as insignificant the question whether such regulations should be issued by Congress or by a bureaucratic agency. They would have easily understood that government control of business is ultimately incompatible with any form of constitutional and democratic government.

It is not an accident that socialist countries are ruled in a dictatorial way. Totalitarianism and government by the people are irreconcilable. Things in Germany and Russia would not be different if Hitler and Stalin were to submit all their decrees to the decision of their "parliaments." Under government control of business parliaments cannot be anything else than assemblies of yes men.

Neither is it justifiable to find fault with the fact that the offices of the bureaucratic administrators are not elective. Election of executives is reasonable only in the case of top executives. Here the voters have to choose among candidates whose political character and convictions they know. It would be absurd to use the same method for the appointment of a host of unknown people. It makes sense if the citizens vote for President, for Governor, or for Mayor. It would be nonsensical to let them vote for the hundreds and thousands of minor clerks. In such elections the voters would have no choice but to endorse the list proposed by their party. It makes no material difference whether the duly elected President or Governor nominates all his aides or whether the voters vote for a list containing the names of all those men whom their preferred candidate has chosen as aides.

It is quite correct, as the opponents of the trend toward totalitarianism say, that the bureaucrats are free to decide according to their own discretion questions of vital importance for the individual citizen's life. It is true that the officeholders are no longer the servants of the citizenry but irresponsible and arbitrary masters and tyrants. But this is not the fault of bureaucracy. It is the outcome of the new system of government which restricts the individual's freedom to manage his own affairs and assigns more and more tasks to the government. The culprit is not the bureaucrat but the political system. And the sovereign people is still free to discard this system.

It is further true that bureaucracy is imbued with an implacable hatred of private business and free enterprise. But the supporters of the system consider precisely this the most laudable feature of their attitude. Far from being ashamed of their anti-business policies, they are proud of them. They aim at full control of business by the government and see in every businessman who wants to evade this control a public enemy.

Finally it is true that the new policy, although not unconstitutional from a merely formalistic viewpoint, is contrary to the spirit of the Constitution, that it is tantamount to an overthrow of all that was precious to the older generations of Americans, that it must result in an abandonment of what people used to call democracy, and that it is in this sense un-American. But this reproach too does not discredit the "progressive" tendencies in the eyes of their supporters. They look at the past with other eyes than their critics'. For them the history of all hitherto existing society is a record of human degradation, misery, and ruthless exploitation of the masses by ruling classes. What is called "individualism" in the American language is, they say, "a

high-sounding term for money greed transfigured and
parading as a virtue." The idea was "to give a free hand
to money-getters, sharp-witted tricksters, stock manipula-
tors and other bandits who lived by raids on the national
income."[1] The American system is scorned as a spurious
"bill-of-rights democracy," and the Russian system of
Stalin is extravagantly praised as the only truly democratic
one.

The main issue in present-day political struggles is
whether society should be organized on the basis of private
ownership of the means of production (capitalism, the
market system) or on the basis of public control of the
means of production (socialism, communism, planned economy). Capitalism means free enterprise, sovereignty of
the consumers in economic matters, and sovereignty of the
voters in political matters. Socialism means full government control of every sphere of the individual's life and
the unrestricted supremacy of the government in its capacity
as central board of production management. There is no
compromise possible between these two systems. Contrary
to a popular fallacy there is no middle way, no third system
possible as a pattern of a permanent social order.[2] The citizens must choose between capitalism and socialism or, as
many Americans say, between the American and the Russian way of life.

Whoever in this antagonism sides with capitalism must
do it frankly and directly. He must give positive support
to private property and free enterprise. It is vain to content
oneself with attacks on some measures designed to pave
the way for socialism. It is useless to fight mere attendant
phenomena and not the tendency toward totalitarianism

1. W. E. Woodward, *A New American History* (New York, 1938), p.
808. On the jacket of this book we read: "Any right-thinking parent today,
conversant with all the facts, would probably find Benedict Arnold in general
far more satisfactory than Lincoln as a pattern for his son." It is obvious that
those who hold such views will not find any fault with the un-Americanism
of bureaucracy.

2. See below pp. 117–119.

as such. It is idle to dwell on a criticism of bureaucratism only.

3. THE "PROGRESSIVES'" VIEW OF BUREAUCRATISM

The "progressive" critics of bureaucratism direct their attacks primarily against the bureaucratization of corporate big business. Their reasoning runs this way:

"In the past business firms were comparatively small. The entrepreneur was in a position to survey all parts of his enterprise and to make all important decisions personally. He was the owner of all the capital invested or at least of the greater part of it. He was himself vitally interested in the success of his enterprise. He was therefore to the best of his abilities intent on making his outfit as efficient as possible and on avoiding waste.

"But with the inexorable trend toward economic concentration, conditions changed radically. Today the scene is dominated by corporate big business. It is absentee ownership; the legal owners, the stockholders, have no actual voice in the management. This task is left to professional administrators. The enterprises are so large that functions and activities must be distributed among departments and administrative subdivisions. The conduct of affairs necessarily becomes bureaucratic.

"The present-day champions of free enterprise are romantics like the eulogists of the medieval arts and crafts. They are entirely mistaken in attributing to mammoth corporations the qualities which once were the excellence of small or medium-size business. There cannot be any question of breaking up the big aggregates into smaller units. On the contrary, the tendency toward a further concentration of economic power will prevail. Monopolized big business will congeal into rigid bureaucratism. Its managers, responsible to nobody, will become a hereditary aristocracy; the governments will become mere puppets of an omnipotent business clique.

"It is indispensable to curb the power of this managerial oligarchy by government action. The complaints about government regimentation are unfounded. As things are, there is only the choice between the rule of an irresponsible managerial bureaucracy and that of the nation's government."

The apologetic character of such reasoning is obvious. To the general criticism of the spread of governmental bureaucratism the "progressives" and New Dealers reply that bureaucracy is not at all limited to government. It is a universal phenomenon present both in business and in government. Its broadest cause is "the tremendous size of the organization." [3] It is therefore an inescapable evil.

This book will try to demonstrate that no profit-seeking enterprise, no matter how large, is liable to become bureaucratic provided the hands of its management are not tied by government interference. The trend toward bureaucratic rigidity is not inherent in the evolution of business. It is an outcome of government meddling with business. It is a result of the policies designed to eliminate the profit motive from its role in the framework of society's economic organization.

In these introductory remarks we want to dwell only upon one point of the popular complaints about the growing bureaucratization of business. Bureaucratization, people say, is caused by "the lack of competent, effective leadership." [4] What is wanting is "creative leadership."

To complain of lack of leadership is, in the field of political affairs, the characteristic attitude of all harbingers of dictatorship. In their eyes the main deficiency of democratic government is that it is unable to produce great Führers and Duces.

In the field of business creative leadership manifests itself in the adjustment of production and distribution to the changing conditions of demand and supply and in the

---

3. Cf. Marshall E. Dimock and Howard K. Hyde, *Bureaucracy and Trusteeship in Large Corporations*, TNEC Monograph No. 11, p. 36.
4. Cf. Dimock and Hyde, *loc. cit.*, p. 44, and the articles quoted by them.

adaptation of technical improvements to practical uses. The great businessman is he who produces more, better, and cheaper goods, who, as a pioneer of progress, presents his fellow men with commodities and services hitherto unknown to them or beyond their means. We may call him a leader because his initiative and activity force his competitors either to emulate his achievements or to go out of business. It is his indefatigable inventiveness and fondness for innovations that prevents all business units from degenerating into idle bureaucratic routine. He embodies in his person the restless dynamism and progressivism inherent in capitalism and free enterprise.

It would certainly be an exaggeration to say that such creative leaders are lacking in present-day America. Many of the old heroes of American business are still alive and active in the conduct of their affairs. It would be a delicate matter to express an opinion about the creativeness of younger men. Some temporal distance is needed for a correct appreciation of their achievements. A true genius is very rarely acknowledged as such by his contemporaries.

Society cannot contribute anything to the breeding and growing of ingenious men. A creative genius cannot be trained. There are no schools for creativeness. A genius is precisely a man who defies all schools and rules, who deviates from the traditional roads of routine and opens up new paths through land inaccessible before. A genius is always a teacher, never a pupil; he is always self-made. He does not owe anything to the favor of those in power. But, on the other hand, the government can bring about conditions which paralyze the efforts of a creative spirit and prevent him from rendering useful services to the community.

This is the case today in the field of business. Let us look at one instance only, the income tax. In the past an ingenious newcomer started a new project. It was a modest start; he was poor, his funds were small and most of them borrowed. When initial success came, he did not increase his consumption, but reinvested the much greater part of the profits. Thus his business grew quickly. He became a leader in his line. His threatening competition forced the old rich firms and the big corporations to adjust their management to the conditions brought about by his intervention. They could not disregard him and indulge in bureaucratic negligence. They were under the necessity of being on their guard day and night against such dangerous innovators. If they could not find a man able to rival the newcomer for the management of their own affairs, they had to merge their own business with his and yield to his leadership.

But today the income tax absorbs 80 or more per cent of such a newcomer's initial profits. He cannot accumulate capital; he cannot expand his business; his enterprise will never become big business. He is no match for the old vested interests. The old firms and corporations already own a considerable capital. Income and corporation taxes prevent them from accumulating more capital, while they prevent the newcomer from accumulating any capital. He is doomed to remain small business forever. The already existing enterprises are sheltered against the dangers from ingenious newcomers. They are not menaced by their competition. They enjoy a virtual privilege as far as they content themselves with keeping their business in the traditional lines and in the traditional size.[5] Their further development, of course, is curtailed. The continuous drain on their profits by taxes makes it impossible for them to expand their business out of their own funds. Thus a tendency toward rigidity originates.

In all countries all tax laws are today written as if the main purpose of taxes were to hinder the accumulation of new capital and the improvements which it could achieve. The same tendency manifests itself in many other branches

---

5. This is not an essay on the social and economic consequences of taxation. Thus there is no need to deal with the effects of the inheritance taxes, the impact of which has already been perceptible in this country for many years, while the above-described effects of the income tax are a recent phenomenon.

of public policy. The "progressives" are badly off the mark when they complain about the lack of creative business leadership. Not the men are lacking but the institutions which would permit them to utilize their gifts. Modern policies result in tying the hands of innovators no less than did the guild system of the Middle Ages.

4. BUREAUCRATISM AND TOTALITARIANISM

It will be shown in this book that bureaucracy and bureaucratic methods are very old and that they must be present in the administrative apparatus of every government the sovereignty of which stretches over a large area. The Pharaohs of ancient Egypt and the emperors of China built a huge bureaucratic machine and so did all the other rulers. Medieval feudalism was an attempt to organize the government of large territories without bureaucrats and bureaucratic methods. It failed utterly in these endeavors. It resulted in a complete disintegration of political unity and in anarchy. The feudal lords, originally officeholders only and as such subject to the authority of the central government, became virtually independent princes, fighting one another almost continually and defying the king, the courts, and the laws. From the fifteenth century on curbing the arrogance of the vassals was the main task of the various European kings. The modern state is built upon the ruins of feudalism. It substituted bureaucratic management of public affairs for the supremacy of a multitude of petty princes and counts.

Far ahead in this evolution were the kings of France. Alexis de Tocqueville has shown how the Bourbon kings unswervingly aimed at the abolition of the autonomy of powerful vassals and of oligarchic groups of aristocrats. In this regard the French Revolution only achieved what the absolute kings themselves had begun. It eliminated the arbitrariness of the kings, it made the law supreme in the field of administration and restricted the scope of affairs subject to the discretionary judgment of the office-holders. It did not brush away bureaucratic management; it only put it on a legal and constitutional basis. France's nineteenth-century administrative system was an attempt to tame the arbitrariness of the bureaucrats as much as possible by law. It served as a model for all other liberal nations which—outside of the realm of Anglo-Saxon Common Law—were anxious to make law and legality paramount in the conduct of civil administration.

It is not sufficiently known that the Prussian administrative system, so much admired by all advocates of government omnipotence, in its early beginnings was but an imitation of French institutions. Frederick II, the "Great" King, imported from royal France not only the methods but even the personnel for their execution. He handed over the administration of the excise duties and the customs to an imported staff of several hundred French bureaucrats. He appointed a Frenchman Postmaster General and another Frenchman President of the Academy. The eighteenth-century Prussians had even better grounds for calling bureaucratism un-Prussian than the present-day Americans for calling it un-American.

The legal technique of administrative activity in the countries of Anglo-Saxon Common Law was very different from that of the continental countries of Europe. Both the British and the Americans were fully convinced that their system gave them a most effective protection against the encroachment of administrative arbitrariness. However, the experience of the last decades has clearly evidenced that no legal precautions are strong enough to resist a trend supported by a powerful ideology. The popular ideas of government interference with business and of socialism have undermined the dams erected by twenty generations of Anglo-Saxons against the flood of arbitrary rule. Many intellectuals and numerous voters organized in the pressure groups of farming and of labor disparage the traditional American system of government as "plutocratic" and yearn for the adoption of the Russian methods which do not accord the individual any protection at all against the discretionary power of the authorities.

Totalitarianism is much more than mere bureaucracy. It is the subordination of every individual's whole life, work, and leisure, to the orders of those in power and office. It is the reduction of man to a cog in an all-embracing machine of compulsion and coercion. It forces the individual to renounce any activity of which the government does not approve. It tolerates no expression of dissent. It is the transformation of society into a strictly disciplined labor-army—as the advocates of socialism say—or into a penitentiary—as its opponents say. At any rate it is the radical break from the way of life to which the civilized nations clung in the past. It is not merely the return of mankind to the oriental despotism under which, as Hegel observed, one man alone was free and all the rest slaves, for those Asiatic kings did not interfere with the daily routine of their subjects. To the individual farmers, cattle breeders, and artisans a field of activities was left in the performance of which they were not troubled by the king and his satellites. They enjoyed some amount of autonomy within their own households and families. It is different with modern socialism. It is totalitarian in the strict sense of the term. It holds the individual in tight rein from the womb to the tomb. At every instant of his life the "comrade" is bound to obey implicitly the orders issued by the supreme authority. The *State* is both his guardian and his employer. The State determines his work, his diet, and his pleasures. The State tells him what to think and what to believe in.

Bureaucracy is instrumental in the execution of these plans. But people are unfair in indicting the individual bureaucrat for the vices of the system. The fault is not with the men and women who fill the offices and bureaus. They are no less the victims of the new way of life than anybody else. The system is bad, not its subordinate handy men. A government cannot do without bureaus and bureaucratic methods. And as social coöperation cannot work without a civil government, some amount of bureaucracy is indispensable. What people resent is not bureaucratism as such, but the intrusion of bureaucracy into all spheres of human life and activity. The struggle against the encroachments of bureaucracy is essentially a revolt against totalitarian dictatorship. It is a misnomer to label the fight for freedom and democracy a fight against bureaucracy.

Nonetheless there is some substance in the general complaint against bureaucratic methods and procedures. For their faults are indicative of the essential defects of any socialist or totalitarian scheme. In thoroughly investigating the problem of bureaucracy we must finally discover why the socialist utopias are entirely impracticable and must, when put into practice, result not only in impoverishment for all but in the disintegration of social coöperation—in chaos. Thus the study of bureaucracy is a good approach to a study of both systems of social organization, capitalism and socialism.

5. THE ALTERNATIVE: PROFIT MANAGEMENT OR BUREAU-CRATIC MANAGEMENT

If we want to find out what bureaucracy really means we must start with an analysis of the operation of the profit motive within the framework of a capitalist society. The essential features of capitalism are no less unknown than those of bureaucracy. Spurious legends, popularized by demagogic propaganda, have entirely misrepresented the capitalist system. Capitalism has succeeded in raising the material well-being of the masses in an unprecedented way. In the capitalist countries population figures are now several times higher than they were at the eve of the "industrial revolution," and every citizen of these nations enjoys a standard of living much higher than that of the well-to-do of earlier ages. Nevertheless a great part of public opinion disparages free enterprise and private ownership of the means of production as dismal institutions that are detrimental to the immense majority of the nation and further only the selfish class interests of a small group of exploiters. Politicians whose main achievement consisted in restricting agricultural output and in attempts to put obstacles in the way of technical improvement of methods of manufacturing discredit capitalism as an "economy of scarcity" and talk about the abundance that socialism will bring about. The heads of labor unions, whose members drive their own motor cars, are enthusiastic in exalting the conditions of the ragged and barefooted Russian proletarians and in praising the freedom that the workers enjoy in Russia where labor unions have been suppressed and strikes are a criminal offense.

There is no need to enter into a detailed scrutiny of these fables. Our intention is neither to praise nor to condemn. We want to know what the two systems in question are, how they work, and how they serve the needs of the people.

In spite of all the vagueness in the use of the term bureaucracy there seems to be unanimity with regard to the distinction between two contrary methods of doing things: the private citizens' way and the way in which the offices of the government and the municipalities are operated. Nobody denies that the principles according to which a police department is operated differ essentially and radically from the principles applied in the conduct of a profit-seeking enterprise. It will therefore be appropriate to begin with an investigation of the methods in use in these two classes of institutions and to compare them with each other.

Bureaucracy, its merits and its demerits, its working and its operation, can be understood only by contrasting it with the operation of the profit motive as it functions in the capitalistic market society.

I

PROFIT MANAGEMENT

I. THE OPERATION OF THE MARKET MECHANISM

CAPITALISM or market economy is that system of social coöperation and division of labor that is based on private ownership of the means of production. The material factors of production are owned by individual citizens, the capitalists and the landowners. The plants and the farms are operated by the entrepreneurs and the farmers, that is, by individuals or associations of individuals who either themselves own the capital and the soil or have borrowed or rented them from the owners. Free enterprise is the characteristic feature of capitalism. The objective of every enterpriser—whether businessman or farmer—is to make profit.

The capitalists, the enterprisers, and the farmers are instrumental in the conduct of economic affairs. They are at the helm and steer the ship. But they are not free to shape its course. They are not supreme, they are steersmen only, bound to obey unconditionally the captain's orders. The captain is the consumer.

Neither the capitalists nor the entrepreneurs nor the farmers determine what has to be produced. The consumers do that. The producers do not produce for their own consumption but for the market. They are intent on selling their products. If the consumers do not buy the goods offered to them, the businessman cannot recover the outlays made. He loses his money. If he fails to adjust his procedure to the wishes of the consumers he will very soon be removed from his eminent position at the helm. Other men who did better in satisfying the demand of the consumers replace him.

The real bosses, in the capitalist system of market economy, are the consumers. They, by their buying and by their abstention from buying, decide who should own the capital and run the plants. They determine what should be produced and in what quantity and quality. Their attitudes result either in profit or in loss for the enterpriser. They make poor men rich and rich men poor. They are no easy bosses. They are full of whims and fancies, changeable and unpredictable. They do not care a whit for past merit. As soon as something is offered to them that they like better or that is cheaper, they desert their old purveyors. With them nothing counts more than their own satisfaction. They bother neither about the vested interests of capitalists nor about the fate of the workers who lose their jobs if as consumers they no longer buy what they used to buy.

What does it mean when we say that the production of a certain commodity A does not pay? It is indicative of the fact that the consumers are not willing to pay the producers of A enough to cover the prices of the required factors of production, while at the same time other producers will find their incomes exceeding their costs of production. The demand of the consumers is instrumental in the allocation of various factors of production to the various branches of manufacturing consumers' goods. The consumers thus decide how much raw material and labor should be used for the manufacturing of A and how much for some other merchandise. It is therefore nonsensical to contrast production for profit and production for use. With the profit motive the enterpriser is compelled to supply the consumers with those goods which they are asking for most urgently. If the enterpriser were not forced to take the profit motive as his guide, he could produce more of A, in spite of the fact that the consumers prefer to get something else. The profit motive is precisely the factor that forces the businessman to provide in the most efficient way those commodities the consumers want to use.

Thus the capitalist system of production is an economic democracy in which every penny gives a right to vote. The consumers are the sovereign people. The capitalists, the entrepreneurs, and the farmers are the people's mandatories. If they do not obey, if they fail to produce, at the lowest possible cost, what the consumers are asking for, they lose their office. Their task is service to the consumer. Profit and loss are the instruments by means of which the consumers keep a tight rein on all business activities.

2. ECONOMIC CALCULATION

The preëminence of the capitalist system consists in the fact that it is the only system of social coöperation and division of labor which makes it possible to apply a method of reckoning and computation in planning new projects and appraising the usefulness of the operation of those plants, farms, and workshops already working. The impracticability of all schemes of socialism and central planning is to be seen in the impossibility of any kind of economic calculation under conditions in which there is no private ownership of the means of production and consequently no market prices for these factors.

The problem to be solved in the conduct of economic affairs is this: There are countless kinds of material factors of production, and within each class they differ from one another both with regard to their physical properties and to the places at which they are available. There are millions and millions of workers and they differ widely with regard to their ability to work. Technology provides us with information about numberless possibilities in regard to what could be achieved by using this supply of natural resources, capital goods, and manpower for the production of consumers' goods. Which of these potential procedures and plans are the most advantageous? Which should be carried out because they are apt to contribute most to the satisfaction of the most urgent needs? Which should be postponed or discarded because their execution would divert factors of production from other projects the execution of which would contribute more to the satisfaction of urgent needs?

It is obvious that these questions cannot be answered by some calculation in kind. One cannot make a variety of things enter into a calculus if there is no common denominator for them.

In the capitalist system all designing and planning is based on the market prices. Without them all the projects and blueprints of the engineers would be a mere academic pastime. They would demonstrate what could be done and how. But they would not be in a position to determine whether the realization of a certain project would really increase material well-being or whether it would not, by withdrawing scarce factors of production from other lines, jeopardize the satisfaction of more urgent needs, that is, of needs considered more urgent by the consumers. The guide of economic planning is the market price. The market prices alone can answer the question whether the execution of a project P will yield more than it costs, that is, whether it will be more useful than the execution of other conceivable plans which cannot be realized because the factors of production required are used for the performance of project P.

It has been frequently objected that this orientation of economic activity according to the profit motive, i.e., according to the yardstick of a surplus of yield over costs, leaves out of consideration the interests of the nation as a whole and takes account only of the selfish interests of individuals, different from and often even contrary to the national interests. This idea lies at the bottom of all totalitarian planning. Government control of business, it is claimed by the advocates of authoritarian management, looks after the nation's well-being, while free enterprise, driven by the sole aim of making profits, jeopardizes national interests.

The case is exemplified nowadays by citing the problem of synthetic rubber. Germany, under the rule of Nazi socialism, has developed the production of synthetic rubber, while Great Britain and the United States, under the supremacy of profit-seeking free enterprise, did not care about the unprofitable manufacture of such an expensive *Ersatz*. Thus they neglected an important item of war preparedness and exposed their independence to a serious danger.

Nothing can be more spurious than this reasoning. Nobody ever asserted that the conduct of a war and preparing a nation's armed forces for the emergency of a war are a task that could or should be left to the activities of individual citizens. The defense of a nation's security and civilization against aggression on the part both of foreign foes and of domestic gangsters is the first duty of any government. If all men were pleasant and virtuous, if no one coveted what belongs to another, there would be no need for a government, for armies and navies, for policemen, for courts, and prisons. It is the government's business to make the provisions for war. No individual citizen and no group or class of citizens are to blame if the government fails in these endeavors. The guilt rests always with the government and consequently, in a democracy, with the majority of voters.

Germany armed for war. As the German General Staff knew that it would be impossible for warring Germany to import natural rubber, they decided to foster domestic production of synthetic rubber. There is no need to inquire whether or not the British and American military authorities were convinced that their countries, even in case of a new World War, would be in a position to rely upon the rubber plantations of Malaya and the Dutch Indies. At any rate they did not consider it necessary to pile up domestic stocks of natural rubber or to embark upon the production of synthetic rubber. Some American and British businessmen examined the progress of synthetic rubber production in Germany. But as the cost of the synthetic product was considerably higher than that of the natural product, they could not venture to imitate the example set by the

Germans. No entrepreneur can invest money in a project which does not offer the prospect of profitability. It is precisely this fact that makes the consumers sovereign and forces the enterpriser to produce what the consumers are most urgently asking for. The consumers, that is, the American and the British public, were not ready to allow for synthetic rubber prices which would have rendered its production profitable. The cheapest way to provide rubber was for the Anglo-Saxon countries to produce other merchandise, for instance, motor cars and various machines, to sell these things abroad, and to import foreign natural rubber.

If it had been possible for the Governments of London and Washington to foresee the events of December, 1941, and January and February, 1942, they would have turned toward measures securing a domestic production of synthetic rubber. It is immaterial with regard to our problem which method they would have chosen for financing this part of defense expenditure. They could subsidize the plants concerned or they could raise, by means of tariffs, the domestic price of rubber to such a level that home production of synthetic rubber would have become profitable. At any rate the people would have been forced to pay for what was done.

If the government does not provide for a defense measure, no capitalist or entrepreneur can fill the gap. To reproach some chemical corporations for not having taken up production of synthetic rubber is no more sensible than to blame the motor industry for not, immediately after Hitler's rise to power, converting its plants into plane factories. Or it would be as justifiable to blame a scholar for having wasted his time writing a book on American history or philosophy instead of devoting all his efforts to training himself for his future functions in the Expeditionary Force. If the government fails in its task of equipping the nation to repel an attack, no individual citizen has any way open to remedy the evil but to criticize the authorities in addressing the sovereign—the voters—in speeches, articles, and books.[1]

Many doctors describe the ways in which their fellow citizens spend their money as utterly foolish and opposed to their real needs. People, they say, should change their diet, restrict their consumption of intoxicating beverages and tobacco, and employ their leisure time in a more reasonable manner. These doctors are probably right. But it is not the task of government to improve the behavior of its "subjects." Neither is it the task of businessmen. They are not the guardians of their customers. If the public prefers hard to soft drinks, the entrepreneurs have to yield to these wishes. He who wants to reform his countrymen must take recourse to persuasion. This alone is the democratic way of bringing about changes. If a man fails in his endeavors to convince other people of the soundness of his ideas, he should blame his own disabilities. He should not ask for a law, that is, for compulsion and coercion by the police.

The ultimate basis of economic calculation is the valuation of all consumers' goods on the part of all the people. It is true that these consumers are fallible and that their judgment is sometimes misguided. We may assume that they would appraise the various commodities differently if they were better instructed. However, as human nature is, we have no means of substituting the wisdom of an infallible authority for people's shallowness.

We do not assert that the market prices are to be considered as expressive of any perennial and absolute value. There are no such things as absolute values, independent of the subjective preferences of erring men. Judgments of value are the outcome of human arbitrariness. They reflect all the shortcomings and weaknesses of their authors. How-

1. These observations do not imply any criticism of the prewar policies pursued by the British and American authorities. Only a man who had knowledge of the military events of 1941–43 many years before they occurred would have the right to blame other people for their lack of foresight. Governments are not omniscient, as the planners would have us believe.

ever, the only alternative to the determination of market prices by the choices of all consumers is the determination of values by the judgment of some small groups of men, no less liable to error and frustration than the majority, notwithstanding the fact that they are called "authority." No matter how the values of consumers' goods are determined, whether they are fixed by a dictatorial decision or by the choices of all consumers—the whole people—values are always relative, subjective, and human, never absolute, objective, and divine.

What must be realized is that within a market society organized on the basis of free enterprise and private ownership of the means of production the prices of consumers' goods are faithfully and closely reflected in the prices of the various factors required for their production. Thus it becomes feasible to discover by means of a precise calculation which of the indefinite multitude of thinkable processes of production are more advantageous and which less. "More advantageous" means in this connection: an employment of these factors of production in such a way that the production of the consumers' goods more urgently asked for by the consumers gets a priority over the production of commodities less urgently asked for by the consumers. Economic calculation makes it possible for business to adjust production to the demands of the consumers. On the other hand, under any variety of socialism, the central board of production management would not be in a position to engage in economic calculation. Where there are no markets and consequently no market prices for the factors of production, they cannot become elements of a calculation.

For a full understanding of the problems involved we must try to grasp the nature and the origin of profit.

Within a hypothetical system without any change there would not be any profits and losses at all. In such a stationary world, in which nothing new occurs and all economic conditions remain permanently the same, the total sum that a manufacturer must spend for the factors of production required would be equal to the price he gets for the product. The prices to be paid for the material factors of production, the wages and interest for the capital invested, would absorb the whole price of the product. Nothing would be left for profit. It is obvious that such a system would not have any need for entrepreneurs and no economic function for profits. As only those things are produced today which were produced yesterday, the day before yesterday, last year, and ten years ago, and as the same routine will go on forever, as no changes occur in the supply or demand either of consumers' or of producers' goods or in technical methods, as all prices are stable, there is no room left for any entrepreneurial activity.

But the actual world is a world of permanent change. Population figures, tastes, and wants, the supply of factors of production and technological methods are in a ceaseless flux. In such a state of affairs there is need for a continuous adjustment of production to the change in conditions. This is where the entrepreneur comes in.

Those eager to make profits are always looking for an opportunity. As soon as they discover that the relation of the prices of the factors of production to the anticipated prices of the products seem to offer such an opportunity, they step in. If their appraisal of all the elements involved was correct, they make a profit. But immediately the tendency toward a disappearance of such profits begins to take effect. As an outcome of the new projects inaugurated, the prices of the factors of production in question go up and, on the other hand, those of the products begin to drop. Profits are a permanent phenomenon only because there are always changes in market conditions and in methods of production. He who wants to make profits must be always on the watch for new opportunities. And in searching for profit, he adjusts production to the demands of the consuming public.

We can view the whole market of material factors of

production and of labor as a public auction. The bidders are the entrepreneurs. Their highest bids are limited by their expectation of the prices the consumers will be ready to pay for the products. The co-bidders competing with them, whom they must outbid if they are not to go away empty-handed, are in the same situation. All these bidders are, as it were, acting as mandatories of the consumers. But each of them represents a different aspect of the consumers' wants, either another commodity or another way of producing the same commodity. The competition among the various entrepreneurs is essentially a competition among the various possibilities open to individuals to remove as far as possible their state of uneasiness by the acquisition of consumers' goods. The resolution of any man to buy a refrigerator and to postpone the purchase of a new car is a determining factor in the formation of the prices of cars and of refrigerators. The competition between the entrepreneurs reflects these prices of consumers' goods in the formation of the prices of the factors of production. The fact that the various wants of the individual, which conflict because of the inexorable scarcity of the factors of production, are represented on the market by various competing entrepreneurs results in prices for these factors that make economic calculation not only feasible but imperative. An entrepreneur who does not calculate, or disregards the result of the calculation, would very soon go bankrupt and be removed from his managerial function.

But within a socialist community in which there is only one manager there are neither prices of the factors of production nor economic calculation. To the entrepreneur of capitalist society a factor of production through its price sends out a warning: Don't touch me, I am earmarked for the satisfaction of another, more urgent need. But under socialism these factors of production are mute. They give no hint to the planner. Technology offers him a great variety of possible solutions for the same problem. Each of them requires the outlay of other kinds and quantities of various factors of production. But as the socialist manager cannot reduce them to a common denominator, he is not in a position to find out which of them is the most advantageous.

It is true that under socialism there would be neither discernible profits nor discernible losses. Where there is no calculation, there is no means of getting an answer to the question whether the projects planned or carried out were those best fitted to satisfy the most urgent needs; success and failure remain unrecognized in the dark. The advocates of socialism are badly mistaken in considering the absence of discernible profit and loss an excellent point. It is, on the contrary, the essential vice of any socialist management. It is not an advantage to be ignorant of whether or not what one is doing is a suitable means of attaining the ends sought. A socialist management would be like a man forced to spend his life blindfolded.

It has been objected that the market system is at any rate quite inappropriate under the conditions brought about by a great war. If the market mechanism were to be left alone, it would be impossible for the government to get all the equipment needed. The scarce factors of production required for the production of armaments would be wasted for civilian uses which, in a war, are to be considered as less important, even as luxury and waste. Thus it was imperative to resort to the system of government-established priorities and to create the necessary bureaucratic apparatus.

The error of this reasoning is that it does not realize that the necessity for giving the government full power to determine for what kinds of production the various raw materials should be used is not an outcome of the war but of the methods applied in financing the war expenditure.

If the whole amount of money needed for the conduct of the war had been collected by taxes and by borrowing from the public, everybody would have been forced to restrict his consumption drastically. With a money income (after taxes) much lower than before, the consumers would have stopped buying many goods they used to buy before the war. The manufacturers, precisely because they are driven by the profit motive, would have discontinued producing such civilian goods and would have shifted to the production of those goods which the government, now by virtue of the inflow of taxes the biggest buyer on the market, would be ready to buy.

However, a great part of the war expenditure is financed by an increase of currency in circulation and by borrowing from the commercial banks. On the other hand, under price control, it is illegal to raise commodity prices. With higher money incomes and with unchanged commodity prices people would not only not have restricted but have increased their buying of goods for their own consumption. To avoid this, it was necessary to take recourse to rationing and to government-imposed priorities. These measures were needed because previous government interference that paralyzed the operation of the market resulted in paradoxical and highly unsatisfactory conditions. Not the insufficiency of the market mechanism but the inadequacy of previous government meddling with market phenomena made the priority system unavoidable. In this as in many other instances the bureaucrats see in the failure of their preceding measures a proof that further inroads into the market system are necessary.

3. MANAGEMENT UNDER THE PROFIT SYSTEM

All business transactions are examined by shrewdly calculating profit and loss. New projects are subject to a precise scrutiny of the chances they offer. Every step toward their realization is reflected in entries in the books and accounts. The profit-and-loss account shows whether or not the whole business, or any of its parts, was profitable. The figures of the ledger serve as a guide for the conduct of the whole business and of each of its divisions. Branches which do not pay are discontinued, those yielding profit are expanded.

There cannot be any question of clinging to unprofitable lines of business if there is no prospect of rendering them profitable in a not-too-distant future.

The elaborate methods of modern bookkeeping, accountancy, and business statistics provide the enterpriser with a faithful image of all his operations. He is in a position to learn how successful or unsuccessful every one of his transactions was. With the aid of these statements he can check the activities of all departments of his concern no matter how large it may be. There is, to be sure, some amount of discretion in determining the distribution of overhead costs. But apart from this, the figures provide a faithful reflection of all that is going on in every branch or department. The books and the balance sheets are the conscience of business. They are also the businessman's compass.

The devices of bookkeeping and accountancy are so familiar to the businessman that he fails to observe what a marvelous instrument they are. It needed a great poet and writer to appreciate them at their true value. Goethe called bookkeeping by double-entry "one of the finest inventions of the human mind." By means of this, he observed, the businessman can at any time survey the general whole, without needing to perplex himself with the details.[2]

Goethe's characterization hit the core of the matter. The virtue of commercial management lies precisely in the fact that it provides the manager with a method of surveying the whole and all its parts without being enmeshed in details and trifles.

The entrepreneur is in a position to separate the calculation of each part of his business in such a way that he can determine the role that it plays within his whole enterprise. For the public every firm or corporation is an undivided unity. But for the eye of its management it is composed of various sections, each of which is viewed as a separate entity and appreciated according to the share it contributes to the

2. *Wilhelm Meister's Apprenticeship*, Book I, chap. X.

success of the whole enterprise. Within the system of business calculation each section represents an integral being, a hypothetical independent business as it were. It is assumed that this section "owns" a definite part of the whole capital employed in the enterprise, that it buys from other sections and sells to them, that it has its own expenses and its own revenues, that its dealings result either in a profit or a loss which is imputed to its own conduct of affairs as separate from the results achieved by the other sections. Thus the general manager of the whole enterprise can assign to each section's management a great deal of independence. There is no need for the general manager to bother about the minor details of each section's management. The managers of the various sections can have a free hand in the administration of their sections' "internal" affairs. The only directive that the general manager gives to the men whom he entrusts with the management of the various sections, departments, and branches is: Make as much profit as possible. And an examination of the accounts shows him how successful or unsuccessful they were in executing the directive.

In a large-scale enterprise many sections produce only parts or half-finished products which are not directly sold but are used by other sections in manufacturing the final product. This fact does not alter the conditions described. The general manager compares the costs incurred by the production of such parts and half-finished products with the prices he would have to pay for them if he had to buy them from other plants. He is always confronted by the question: Does it pay to produce these things in our own workshops? Would it not be more satisfactory to buy them from other plants specializing in their production?

Thus within the framework of a profit-seeking enterprise responsibility can be divided. Every submanager is responsible for the working of his department. It is to his credit if the accounts show a profit, and it is to his disadvantage if they show a loss. His own selfish interests push him toward the utmost care and exertion in the conduct of his section's affairs. If he incurs losses, he will be their victim. He will be replaced by another man whom the general manager expects to be more successful, or the whole section will be discontinued. At any rate he will be discharged and lose his job. If he succeeds in making profits, he will see his income increased or at least he will not be in danger of losing it. Whether or not a departmental manager is entitled to a share in the profit of his department is not so important with regard to the personal interest he takes in the results of his department's dealings. His fate is at any rate closely connected with that of his department. In working for it, he works not only for his boss but also for himself.

It would be impracticable to restrict the discretion of such a responsible submanager by too much interference with detail. If he is efficient, such meddling would at best be superfluous, if not harmful by tying his hands. If he is inefficient, it would not render his activities more successful. It would only provide him with a lame excuse that the failure was caused by his superior's inappropriate instructions. The only instruction required is self-understood and does not need to be especially mentioned: seek profit. Moreover, most of the details can and must be left to the head of every department.

This system was instrumental in the evolution of modern business. Large-scale production in great production aggregates and the establishment of subsidiaries in distant parts of the country and in foreign countries, the department stores, and the chain stores are all built upon the principle of the subordinate managers' responsibility. This does not in any way limit the responsibility of the general manager. The subordinates are responsible only to him. They do not free him from the duty of finding the right man for every job.

If a New York firm establishes branch shops or plants

in Los Angeles, in Buenos Aires, in Budapest, and in Calcutta, the chief manager establishes the auxiliary's relation to the head office or parental company only in fairly general terms. All minor questions are to be within the range of the local manager's duties. The auditing department of headquarters carefully inspects the branch's financial transactions and informs the general manager as soon as any irregularities appear. Precautions are taken to prevent irreparable waste of the capital invested in the branch, a squandering of the whole concern's good will and reputation and a collision between the branch's policy and that of headquarters. But a free hand is left to the local management in every other regard. It is practicable to place confidence in the chief of a subsidiary, a department, or a section because his interests and those of the whole concern coincide. If he were to spend too much for current operations or to neglect an opportunity for profitable transactions, he would imperil not only the concern's profits but his own position as well. He is not simply a hired clerk whose only duty is the conscientious accomplishment of an assigned, definite task. He is a businessman himself, a junior partner as it were of the entrepreneur, no matter what the contractual and financial terms of his employment are. He must to the best of his abilities contribute to the success of the firm with which he is connected.

Because this is so, there is no danger in leaving important decisions to his discretion. He will not waste money in the purchase of products and services. He will not hire incompetent assistants and workers; he will not discharge able collaborators in order to replace them by incompetent personal friends or relatives. His conduct is subject to the incorruptible judgment of an unbribable tribunal: the account of profit and loss. In business there is only one thing that matters: success. The unsuccessful department manager is doomed no matter whether the failure was caused by him or not, or whether it would have been possible for him to attain a more satisfactory result. An unprofitable branch of business—sooner or later—must be discontinued, and its manager loses his job.

The sovereignty of the consumers and the democratic operation of the market do not stop at the doors of a big business concern. They permeate all its departments and branches. Responsibility to the consumer is the lifeblood of business and enterprise in an unhampered market society. The profit motive through the instrumentality of which the entrepreneurs are driven to serve the consumers to the best of their ability is at the same time the first principle of any commercial and industrial aggregate's internal organization. It joins together utmost centralization of the whole concern with almost complete autonomy of the parts, it brings into agreement full responsibility of the central management with a high degree of interest and incentive of the subordinate managers of sections, departments, and auxiliaries. It gives to the system of free enterprise that versatility and adaptability which result in an unswerving tendency toward improvement.

4. PERSONNEL MANAGEMENT UNDER AN UNHAMPERED LABOR MARKET

The staff of a modern large-scale enterprise sometimes includes many hundreds of thousands of clerks and workers. They form a highly differentiated body from the general manager or president down to the scrubwomen, messenger boys, and apprentices. The handling of such a huge body raises many problems. However, they can be solved.

No matter how big a concern may be, the central management deals only with sections, departments, branches, and subsidiaries, the role of which can be precisely determined from the evidence provided by the accounts and statistics. Of course, the accounts do not always demonstrate what may be wrong with a section. They show only that something is wrong, that it does not pay, and must be either reformed or discontinued. The sentences they pass are unappealable. They reveal each department's cash value. And it is cash value alone that matters on the market. The consumers are merciless. They never buy in order to benefit a less efficient producer and to protect him against the consequences of his failure to manage better. They want to be served as well as possible. And the working of the capitalist system forces the entrepreneur to obey the orders issued by the consumers. He does not have the power to distribute bounties at the expense of the consumers. He would waste his funds if he were to use his own money for such a purpose. He simply cannot pay anybody more than he can realize in selling the product.

The same relation that exists between the general manager and his immediate subordinates, the heads of the various sections, pervades the whole business hierarchy. Every section head values his immediate subordinates according to the same principle by which the chief manager values him, and the foreman applies similar methods in appraising his subordinates. The only difference is that under the simpler conditions of the lower units no elaborate accountancy schemes are required for the establishment of each man's cash value. It does not matter whether piece wages or hourly wages are paid. In the long run the worker can never get more than the consumer allows.

No man is infallible. It often happens that a superior errs in judging a subordinate. One of the qualifications required for any higher position is precisely the ability to judge people correctly. He who fails in this regard jeopardizes his chances of success. He hurts his own interests no less than those of the men whose efficiency he has underrated. Things being so, there is no need to look for special protection for the employees against arbitrariness on the part of their employers or their employer's mandatories. Arbitrariness in dealing with personnel is, under the unhampered profit system, an offense that strikes home to its author.

Under an unhampered market economy the appraisal of each individual's effort is detached from any personal considerations and can therefore be free both from bias and dislike. The market passes judgment on the products, not on the producers. The appraisal of the producer results automatically from the appraisal of his product. Each co-operator is valued according to the value of his contribution to the process of production of goods and services. Salaries and wages do not depend on arbitrary decisions. On the labor market every quantity and quality of work is prized to the amount the consumers are ready to pay for the products. It is not a favor on the part of the employer to pay wages and salaries, it is a business transaction, the purchase of a factor of production. The price of labor is a market phenomenon determined by the consumers' demands for goods and services. Virtually every employer is always in search of cheaper labor and every employee in search of a job with higher remuneration.

The very fact that labor is, under capitalism, a commodity and is bought and sold as a commodity makes the wage earner free from any personal dependence. Like the capitalists, the entrepreneurs, and the farmers, the wage earner depends on the arbitrariness of the consumers. But the consumers' choices do not concern the persons engaged in production; they concern things and not men. The employer is not in a position to indulge in favoritism or in prejudice with regard to personnel. As far as he does, the deed itself brings about its own penalty.

It is this fact, and not only constitutions and bills of rights, that makes the receivers of salaries and wages *within an unhampered capitalist system* free men. They are sovereign in their capacity as consumers, and as producers they are, like all other citizens, unconditionally subject to the law of the market. In selling a factor of production, namely, their toil and trouble, on the market at the market price to everybody who is ready to buy it, they do not jeopardize their own standing. They do not owe their employer thanks and subservience, they owe him a definite quantity of labor of a definite quality. The employer, on the other hand, is not in search of sympathetic men whom he likes but efficient workers who are worth the money he pays them.

This cool rationality and objectivity of capitalist relations is, of course, not realized to the same degree in the whole field of business. The nearer a man's function brings him to the consumers, the more personal factors interfere. In the service trades some role is played by sympathies and antipathies; relations are more "human." Stubborn doctrinaires and adamant baiters of capitalism are prepared to call this an advantage. In fact it curtails the businessman's and his employees' personal freedom. A small shopkeeper, a barber, an innkeeper, and an actor are not so free in expressing their political or religious convictions as the owner of a cotton mill or a worker in a steel plant.

But these facts do not invalidate the general characteristics of the market system. It is a system which automatically values every man according to the services he renders to the body of sovereign consumers, i.e., to his fellow men.

II

BUREAUCRATIC MANAGEMENT

THE chieftain of a small primitive tribe is as a rule in a position to concentrate in his hands all legislative, administrative, and judiciary power. His will is the law. He is both executive and judge.

But it is different when the despot has succeeded in expanding the size of his realm. As he lacks ubiquity, he must delegate a part of his power to subordinates. They are, in their districts, his deputies, acting in his name and under his auspices. In fact they become local despots only nominally subject to the mighty overlord who has appointed them. They rule their provinces according to their own will, they become satraps. The great king has the power to discharge them and to appoint a successor. But that is no remedy either. The new governor also soon becomes an almost independent satrap. What some critics—wrongly— assert with regard to representative democracy, namely, that the people is sovereign only on election day, is literally true with regard to such a system of despotism; the king is sovereign in the provinces only on the day he appoints a new governor.

In what does the position of such a provincial governor differ from that of the manager of a business branch? The manager of the whole concern hands over an aggregate to the newly appointed branch manager and gives him one directive only: Make profits. This order, the observance of which is continuously checked by the accounts, is sufficient to make the branch a subservient part of the whole concern and to give to its manager's action the direction aimed at by the central manager. But if the despot, for whom his own arbitrary decision is the only principle of government, appoints a governor and says to him: "Be my deputy in this province," he makes the deputy's arbitrariness supreme in this province. He renounces, at least temporarily, his own power to the benefit of the governor.

In order to avoid this outcome the king tries to limit the governor's powers by issuing directives and instructions. Codes, decrees, and statutes tell the governors of the provinces and their subordinates what to do if such or such a problem arises. Their free discretion is now limited; their first duty is now to comply with the regulations. It is true that their arbitrariness is now restricted in so far as the regulations must be applied. But at the same time the whole character of their management changes. They are no longer eager to deal with each case to the best of their abilities; they are no longer anxious to find the most appropriate solution for every problem. Their main concern is to comply with the rules and regulations, no matter whether they are reasonable or contrary to what was intended. The first virtue of an administrator is to abide by the codes and decrees. He becomes a bureaucrat.

2. BUREAUCRACY WITHIN A DEMOCRACY

The same thing is essentially valid for democratic government.

It is frequently asserted that bureaucratic management is incompatible with democratic government and institutions. This is a fallacy. Democracy implies the supremacy of the law. If it were otherwise, the officeholders would be irresponsible and arbitrary despots and the judges inconstant and capricious cadis. The two pillars of democratic government are the primacy of the law and the budget.[1]

1. This is not a definition of democratic government but a description of the administrative technique of democratic government. The definition of democratic government is: A system of government under which those ruled are in a position to determine, directly by plebiscite or indirectly by election, the exercise of the legislative and executive power and the selection of the supreme executives.

Primacy of the law means that no judge or officeholder has the right to interfere with any individual's affairs or conditions unless a valid law requires or empowers him to do so. *Nulla poena sine lege,* no punishment unless ordered by a law. It is precisely the inability of the Nazis to understand the importance of this fundamental principle that qualifies them as antidemocratic. In the totalitarian system of Hitler Germany the judge has to come to his decision according to *das gesunde Volksempfinden,* i.e., in accordance with the sound feelings of the people. As the judge himself has to decide what the sound feelings of the people are, he is sovereign on his bench like the chieftain of a primitive tribe.

It is in fact an awkward thing if a scoundrel evades punishment because a law is defective. But it is the minor evil when compared with judicial arbitrariness. If the legislators acknowledge that the law is inadequate they can substitute a more satisfactory law for a less satisfactory. They are the mandatories of the sovereign, the people; they are, in this capacity, supreme and responsible to the voters. If the voters disapprove of the methods applied by their representatives, they will, at the next election, return other men who know better how to adjust their actions to the will of the majority.

It is the same with the executive power. In this field too there is only the alternative between the arbitrary rule of despotic officeholders and the rule of the people enforced by the instrumentality of law abidance. It is a euphemism to call a government in which the rulers are free to do whatever they themselves believe best serves the commonweal a *welfare state,* and to contrast it with the state in which the administration is bound by law and the citizens can make good in a court of law their rights against illegal encroachments of the authorities. This so-called welfare state is in fact the tyranny of the rulers. (Incidentally we have to realize that even a despotic government cannot do without regulations and bureaucratic directives if it is not to degenerate into a chaotic regime of local caciques and to disintegrate into a multitude of petty despotisms.) The aim of the constitutional state also is public welfare. The characteristic feature that distinguishes it from despotism is that not the authorities but the duly elected people's representatives have to decide what best serves the commonweal. This system alone makes the people sovereign and secures their right of self-determination. Under this system the citizens are not only sovereign on election day but no less so between elections.

The administration, in a democratic community, is not only bound by law but by the budget. Democratic control is budgetary control. The people's representatives have the keys of the treasury. Not a penny must be spent without the consent of parliament. It is illegal to use public funds for any expenditures other than those for which parliament has allocated them.

Bureaucratic management means, under democracy, management in strict accordance with the law and the budget. It is not for the personnel of the administration and for the judges to inquire what should be done for the public welfare and how the public funds should be spent. This is the task of the sovereign, the people, and their representatives. The courts, the various branches of the administration, the army, and the navy execute what the law and the budget order them to do. Not they but the sovereign is policy-making.

Most of the tyrants, despots, and dictators are sincerely convinced that their rule is beneficial for the people, that theirs is government *for the people*. There is no need to investigate whether these claims of Messrs. Hitler, Stalin, and Franco are well founded or not. At any rate their system is neither government *of the people* nor *by the people*. It is not democratic but authoritarian.

The assertion that bureaucratic management is an indispensable instrument of democratic government is paradoxical. Many will object. They are accustomed to consider democratic government as the best system of government and bureaucratic management as one of the great evils. How can these two things, one good, the other bad, be linked together?

Moreover, America is an old democracy and the talk about the dangers of bureaucracy is a new phenomenon in this country. Only in recent years have people become aware of the menace of bureaucracy, and they consider bureaucracy not an instrument of democratic government but, on the contrary, the worst enemy of freedom and democracy.

To these objections we must answer again that bureaucracy in itself is neither good nor bad. It is a method of management which can be applied in different spheres of human activity. There is a field, namely, the handling of the apparatus of government, in which bureaucratic methods are required by necessity. What many people nowadays consider an evil is not bureaucracy as such, but the expansion of the sphere in which bureaucratic management is applied. This expansion is the unavoidable consequence of the progressive restriction of the individual citizen's freedom, of the inherent trend of present-day economic and social policies toward the substitution of government control for private initiative. People blame bureaucracy, but what they really have in mind are the endeavors to make the state socialist and totalitarian.

There has always been bureaucracy in America. The administration of the customs and of the foreign service has always been conducted according to bureaucratic principles. What characterizes our time is the expansion of the sphere of government interference with business and with many other items of the citizenry's affairs. And this results in a substitution of bureaucratic management for profit management.

3. THE ESSENTIAL FEATURES OF BUREAUCRATIC MANAGEMENT

The lawyers, the philosophers, and the politicians look upon the supremacy of the law from another angle than does this book. From their point of view the main function of the law is to limit the power of the authorities and the courts to inflict evils upon the individual citizen and to restrict his freedom. If one assigns to the authorities the power to imprison or even to kill people, one must restrict and clearly circumscribe this power. Otherwise the officeholder or judge would turn into an irresponsible despot. The law determines under what conditions the judge should have the right and the duty to sentence and the policeman to fire his gun. The law protects the people against the arbitrariness of those in office.

The viewpoint of this book is somewhat different. We are dealing here with bureaucracy as a principle of administrative technique and organization. This book looks upon the rules and regulations not merely as measures for the protection of the people and for safeguarding the citizen's rights and freedom but as measures for the execution of the will of the supreme authority. The need to limit the discretion of subordinates is present in every organization. Any organization would disintegrate in the absence of such restrictions. Our task is to investigate the peculiar characteristics of bureaucratic management as distinguished from commercial management.

Bureaucratic management is management bound to comply with detailed rules and regulations fixed by the authority of a superior body. The task of the bureaucrat is to perform what these rules and regulations order him to do. His discretion to act according to his own best conviction is seriously restricted by them.

Business management or profit management is management directed by the profit motive. The objective of business management is to make a profit. As success or failure to attain this end can be ascertained by accounting not only for the whole business concern but also for any of its parts, it is feasible to decentralize both management and accountability without jeopardizing the unity of operations and the attainment of their goal. Responsibility can be divided. There is no need to limit the discretion of subordinates by any rules or regulations other than that underlying all business activities, namely, to render their operations profitable.

The objectives of public administration cannot be measured in money terms and cannot be checked by accountancy methods. Take a nation-wide police system like the F.B.I. There is no yardstick available that could establish whether the expenses incurred by one of its regional or local branches were not excessive. The expenditures of a police station are not reimbursed by its successful management and do not vary in proportion to the success attained. If the head of the whole bureau were to leave his subordinate station chiefs a free hand with regard to money expenditure, the result would be a large increase in costs as every one of them would be zealous to improve the service of his branch as much as possible. It would become impossible for the top executive to keep the expenditures within the appropriations allocated by the representatives of the people or within any limits whatever. It is not because of punctiliousness that the administrative regulations fix how much can be spent by each local office for cleaning the premises, for furniture repairs, and for lighting and heating. Within a business concern such things can be left without hesitation to the discretion of the responsible local manager. He will not spend more than necessary because it is, as it were, his money; if he wastes the concern's money, he jeopardizes the branch's profit and thereby indirectly hurts his own interests. But it is another matter with the local chief of a government agency. In spending more money he can, very often at least, improve the result of his conduct of affairs. Thrift must be imposed on him by regimentation.

In public administration there is no connection between revenue and expenditure. The public services are spending money only; the insignificant income derived from special sources (for example, the sale of printed matter by the Government Printing Office) is more or less accidental. The revenue derived from customs and taxes is not "produced" by the administrative apparatus. Its source is the law, not the activities of customs officers and tax collectors. It is not the merit of a collector of internal revenue that the residents of his district are richer and pay higher taxes than those of another district. The time and effort required for the administrative handling of an income tax return are not in proportion to the amount of the taxable income it concerns.

In public administration there is no market price for achievements. This makes it indispensable to operate public offices according to principles entirely different from those applied under the profit motive.

Now we are in a position to provide a definition of bureaucratic management: Bureaucratic management is the method applied in the conduct of administrative affairs the result of which has no cash value on the market. Remember: we do not say that a successful handling of public affairs has no value, but that it has no price on the market, that its value cannot be realized in a market transaction and consequently cannot be expressed in terms of money.

If we compare the conditions of two countries, say Atlantis and Thule, we can establish many important statistical figures of each of them: the size of the area and of the population, the birth rate and the death rate, the number of illiterates, of crimes committed, and many other demographical data. We can determine the sum of the money income of all its citizens, the money value of the yearly social product, the money value of the goods imported and exported, and many other economic data. But we cannot assign any arithmetical value to the system of government and administration. That does not mean that we deny the importance or the value of good government. It means only that no yardstick can measure these things. They are not liable to an expression in figures.

It may well be that the greatest thing in Atlantis is its good system of government. It may be that Atlantis owes its prosperity to its constitutional and administrative institutions. But we cannot compare them with those of Thule in the same way as we can compare other things, for instance, wage rates or milk prices.

Bureaucratic management is management of affairs which cannot be checked by economic calculation.

4. THE CRUX OF BUREAUCRATIC MANAGEMENT

The plain citizen compares the operation of the bureaus with the working of the profit system, which is more familiar to him. Then he discovers that bureaucratic management is wasteful, inefficient, slow, and rolled up in red tape. He simply cannot understand how reasonable people allow such a mischievous system to endure. Why not adopt the well-tried methods of private business?

However, such criticisms are not sensible. They misconstrue the features peculiar to public administration. They are not aware of the fundamental difference between government and profit-seeking private enterprise. What they call deficiencies and faults of the management of administrative agencies are necessary properties. A bureau is not a profit-seeking enterprise; it cannot make use of any economic calculation; it has to solve problems which are unknown to business management. It is out of the question to improve its management by reshaping it according to the pattern of private business. It is a mistake to judge the efficiency of a government department by comparing it with the working of an enterprise subject to the interplay of market factors.

There are, of course, in every country's public administration manifest shortcomings which strike the eye of every observer. People are sometimes shocked by the degree of maladministration. But if one tries to go to their roots, one often learns that they are not simply the result of culpable negligence or lack of competence. They sometimes turn out to be the result of special political and institutional conditions or of an attempt to come to an arrangement with a problem for which a more satisfactory solution could not be found. A detailed scrutiny of all the difficulties involved may convince an honest investigator that, given the general state of political forces, he himself would not have known how to deal with the matter in a less objectionable way.

It is vain to advocate a bureaucratic reform through the appointment of businessmen as heads of various departments. The quality of being an entrepreneur is not inherent in the personality of the entrepreneur; it is inherent in the position which he occupies in the framework of market society. A former entrepreneur who is given charge of a government bureau is in this capacity no longer a businessman but a bureaucrat. His objective can no longer be profit, but compliance with the rules and regulations. As head of a bureau he may have the power to alter some minor rules and some matters of internal procedure. But the setting of the bureau's activities is determined by rules and regulations which are beyond his reach.

It is a widespread illusion that the efficiency of government bureaus could be improved by management engineers and their methods of scientific management. However, such plans stem from a radical misconstruction of the objectives of civil government.

Like any kind of engineering, management engineering too is conditioned by the availability of a method of calculation. Such a method exists in profit-seeking business. Here the profit-and-loss statement is supreme. The problem of bureaucratic management is precisely the absence of such a method of calculation.

In the field of profit-seeking enterprise the objective of the management engineer's activities is clearly determined by the primacy of the profit motive. His task is to reduce costs without impairing the market value of the result or to reduce costs more than the ensuing reduction of the market value of the result or to raise the market value of the result more than the required rise in costs. But in the field of government the result has no price on a market. It can neither be bought nor sold.

Let us consider three examples.

A police department has the job of protecting a defense plant against sabotage. It assigns thirty patrolmen to this duty. The responsible commissioner does not need the advice of an efficiency expert in order to discover that he could save money by reducing the guard to only twenty men. But the question is: Does this economy outweigh the increase in risk? There are serious things at stake: national defense, the morale of the armed forces and of civilians, repercussions in the field of foreign affairs, the lives of many upright workers. All these valuable things cannot be assessed in terms of money. The responsibility rests entirely with Congress allocating the appropriations required and with the executive branch of the Government. They cannot evade it by leaving the decision to an irresponsible adviser.

One of the tasks of the Bureau of Internal Revenue is the final determination of taxes due. Its duty is the interpretation and application of the law. This is not merely a clerical job; it is a kind of judicial function. Any taxpayer objecting to the Commissioner's interpretation of the law is free to bring suit in a Federal court to recover the amount paid. Of what use can the efficiency engineer with his time and motion studies be for the conduct of these affairs? His stop watch would be in the wrong place in the office rooms of the bureau. It is obvious that—other things being equal—a clerk who works more quickly is a more desirable employee than another who is slower. But the main problem is the quality of the performance. Only the experienced senior clerks are in a position to appreciate duly the achievements of their aides. Intellectual work cannot be measured and valued by mechanical devices.

Let us finally consider an instance in which neither problems of "higher" politics nor those of the correct application of the law are involved. A bureau is in charge of buying all the supplies needed for the technical conduct of office work. This is a comparatively simple job. But it is by no means a mechanical job. The best clerk is not he who fills out the greatest number of orders in an hour. The most satisfactory performance is to buy the most appropriate materials at the cheapest price.

It is therefore, as far as the management of government is concerned, not correct to assert that time study, motion study, and other tools of scientific management "show with reasonable accuracy how much time and effort are required for each of the available methods" and that they therefore "can show which of the possible methods and procedures require the least time and effort." [2] All such things are quite useless because they cannot be coördinated to the quality of the work done. Speed alone is not a measure of intellectual work. You cannot "measure" a doctor according to the time he employs in examining one case. And you cannot "measure" a judge according to the time he needs to adjudicate one case.

If a businessman manufactures some article destined for export into foreign countries, he is eager to reduce the man-hours spent for the production of the various parts of the commodity in question. But the license required for shipping this commodity abroad is not a part of the commodity. The government in issuing a license does not contribute anything to the production, the marketing, and the shipping of this commodity. Its bureau is not a workshop turning out one of the parts needed for the finishing of the product. What the government aims at in making exports depend on the grant of a license is restraint of export trade. It

2. J. M. Juran, *Bureaucracy, a Challenge to Better Management* (New York, 1944), p. 75.

wants to reduce the total volume of exports or the volume exported by undesirable exporters or sold to undesirable buyers. The issuance of licenses is not the objective but a technical device for its attainment. From the point of view of the government the licenses refused or not even applied for are more important than those granted. It would therefore not be to the purpose to take "the total man-hours spent per license" as the standard of the bureau's performance. It would be unsuitable to perform "the operation of processing the licenses . . . on an assembly line basis." [3]

There are other differences. If in the course of a manufacturing process a piece gets spoiled or lost, the result is a precisely limited increase in production costs. But if a license application is lost in the bureau, serious damage may be inflicted upon a citizen. The law may prevent the individual harmed from suing the bureau for indemnification. But the political and moral liability of the government to deal with these applications in a very careful way remains nonetheless.

The conduct of government affairs is as different from the industrial processes as is prosecuting, convicting, and sentencing a murderer from the growing of corn or the manufacturing of shoes. Government efficiency and industrial efficiency are entirely different things. A factory's management cannot be improved by taking a police department for its model, and a tax collector's office cannot become more efficient by adopting the methods of a motor-car plant. Lenin was mistaken in holding up the government's bureaus as a pattern for industry. But those who want to make the management of the bureaus equal to that of the factories are no less mistaken.

There are many things about government administration which need to be reformed. Of course, all human institutions must again and again be adjusted anew to the change of conditions. But no reform could transform a public of-

3. J. M. Juran, *loc. cit.*, pp. 34, 76.

fice into a sort of private enterprise. A government is not a profit-seeking enterprise. The conduct of its affairs cannot be checked by profit-and-loss statements. Its achievement cannot be valued in terms of money. This is fundamental for any treatment of the problems of bureaucracy.

5. BUREAUCRATIC PERSONNEL MANAGEMENT

A bureaucrat differs from a nonbureaucrat precisely because he is working in a field in which it is impossible to appraise the result of a man's effort in terms of money. The nation spends money for the upkeep of the bureaus, for the payment of salaries and wages, and for the purchase of all the equipment and materials needed. But what it gets for the expenditure, the service rendered, cannot be appraised in terms of money, however important and valuable this "output" may be. Its appraisal depends on the discretion of the government.

It is true that the appraisal of the various commodities sold and bought on the market depends no less on discretion, that is, on the discretion of the consumers. But as the consumers are a vast body of different people, an anonymous and amorphous aggregation, the judgments they pass are congealed into an impersonal phenomenon, the market price, and are thus severed from their arbitrary origin. Moreover, they refer to commodities and services as such, not to their performers. The seller-buyer nexus as well as the employer-employee relation, in profit-seeking business are purely matter of fact and impersonal. It is a deal from which both parties derive an advantage. They mutually contribute to each other's living. But it is different with a bureaucratic organization. There the nexus between superior and subordinate is personal. The subordinate depends on the superior's judgment of his personality, not of his work. As long as the office clerk can rely on his chances of getting a job with private business, this dependence cannot become so oppressive as to mark the clerk's whole character. But it is different under the present trend toward general bureaucratization.

The American scene until a few years ago did not know the bureaucrat as a particular type of human being. There were always bureaus and they were, by necessity, operated in a bureaucratic way. But there was no numerous class of men who considered work in the public offices their exclusive calling. There was a continuous change of personnel between government jobs and private jobs. Under civil service provisions public service became a regular career. Appointments were based on examinations and no longer depended on the political affiliation of the applicants. Many remained in public bureaus for life. But they retained their personal independence because they could always consider a return to private jobs.

It was different in continental Europe. There the bureaucrats have long formed an integrated group. Only for a few eminent men was a return to nonofficial life practically open. The majority were tied up with the bureaus for life. They developed a character peculiar to their permanent removal from the world of profit-seeking business. Their intellectual horizon was the hierarchy and its rules and regulations. Their fate was to depend entirely on the favor of their superiors. They were subject to their sway not only when on duty. It was understood that their private activities also—and even those of their wives—had to be appropriate to the dignity of their position and to a special —unwritten—code of conduct becoming to a *Staatsbeamter* or *fonctionnaire*. It was expected that they would endorse the political viewpoint of the cabinet ministers who happened at the time to be in office. At any rate their freedom to support a party of opposition was sensibly curtailed.

The emergence of a large class of such men dependent on the government became a serious menace to the maintenance of constitutional institutions. Attempts were made to protect the individual clerk against arbitrariness on the part of his superiors. But the only result achieved was that discipline was relaxed and that looseness in the performance of the duties spread more and more.

America is a novice in the field of bureaucracy. It has much less experience in this matter than the classical countries of bureaucracy, France, Germany, Austria, and Russia, acquired. In the United States there still prevails a leaning toward an overvaluation of the usefulness of civil-service regulations. Such regulations require that the applicants be a certain age, graduate from certain schools, and pass certain examinations. For promotion to higher ranks and higher salary a certain number of years spent in the lower ranks and the passing of further examinations are required. It is obvious that all such requirements refer to things more or less superficial. There is no need to point out that school attendance, examinations, and years spent in the lower positions do not necessarily qualify a man for a higher job. This machinery for selection sometimes bars the most competent men from a job and does not always prevent the appointment of an utter incompetent. But the worst effect produced is that the main concern of the clerks is to comply with these and other formalities. They forget that their job is to perform an assigned duty as well as possible.

In a properly arranged civil-service system the promotion to higher ranks depends primarily on seniority. The heads of the bureaus are for the most part old men who know that after a few years they will be retired. Having spent the greater part of their lives in subordinate positions, they have lost vigor and initiative. They shun innovations and improvements. They look on every project for reform as a disturbance of their quiet. Their rigid conservatism frustrates all endeavors of a cabinet minister to adjust the service to changed conditions. They look down upon the cabinet minister as an inexperienced layman. In all countries with a settled bureaucracy people used to say: The cabinets come and go, but the bureaus remain.

It would be a mistake to ascribe the frustration of European bureaucratism to intellectual and moral deficiencies of the personnel. In all these countries there were many good families whose scions chose the bureaucratic career because they were honestly intent on serving their nation. The ideal of a bright poor boy who wanted to attain a better station in life was to join the staff of the administration. Many of the most gifted and lofty members of the intelligentsia served in the bureaus. The prestige and the social standing of the government clerks surpassed by far those of any other class of the population with the exception of the army officers and the members of the oldest and wealthiest aristocratic families.

Many civil servants published excellent treatises dealing with the problems of administrative law and statistics. Some of them were in their leisure hours brilliant writers or musicians. Others entered the field of politics and became eminent party leaders. Of course, the bulk of the bureaucrats were rather mediocre men. But it cannot be doubted that a considerable number of able men were to be found in the ranks of the government employees.

The failure of European bureaucracy was certainly not due to incapacities of the personnel. It was an outcome of the unavoidable weakness of any administration of public affairs. The lack of standards which could, in an unquestionable way, ascertain success or nonsuccess in the performance of an official's duties creates insoluble problems. It kills ambition, destroys initiative and the incentive to do more than the minimum required. It makes the bureaucrat look at instructions, not at material and real success.

III

BUREAUCRATIC MANAGEMENT OF PUBLICLY OWNED ENTERPRISES

1. THE IMPRACTICABILITY OF GOVERNMENT ALL-ROUND CONTROL

SOCIALISM, that is, full government control of all economic activities, is impracticable because a socialist community would lack the indispensable intellectual instrument of economic planning and designing: economic calculation. The very idea of central planning by the state is self-contradictory. A socialist central board of production management will be helpless in the face of the problems to be solved. It will never know whether the projects considered are advantageous or whether their performance would not bring about a waste of the means available. Socialism must result in complete chaos.

The recognition of this truth has for many years been prevented by the taboos of Marxism. One of Marxism's main contributions to the success of pro-socialist propaganda was to outlaw the study of the economic problems of a socialist commonwealth. Such studies were in the opinion of Karl Marx and his sect the mark of an illusory "utopianism." "Scientific" socialism, as Marx and Engels called their own brand, must not indulge in such useless investigations. The "scientific" socialists have to satisfy themselves with the insight that socialism is bound to come and that it will transform the earth into a paradise. They must not be so preposterous as to ask how the socialist system will work.

One of the most remarkable facts of the intellectual history of the nineteenth and early twentieth centuries is that this Marxian *Verboten* was strictly obeyed. The few economists who dared to defy it were disregarded and soon fell into oblivion. Only about twenty-five years ago the spell was broken. The impossibility of economic calculation under socialism was demonstrated in an irrefutable way.

Of course, some stubborn Marxians raised objections. They could not help admitting that the problem of economic calculation was the most serious issue of socialism and that it was a scandal that the socialists in eighty years of fanatical propaganda wasted their time on trifles without divining in what the main problem consisted. But they assured their alarmed partisans that it would be easy to find a satisfactory solution. Indeed, various socialist professors and writers both in Russia and in the Western countries suggested schemes for an economic calculation under socialism. These schemes proved utterly spurious. It was not difficult for the economists to unmask their fallacies and contradictions. The socialists failed completely in their desperate attempts to reject the demonstration that no economic calculation is feasible in any system of socialism.[1]

It is obvious that a socialist management also would aim at supplying the community with as many and as good commodities as can be produced under the existing conditions of the supply of factors of production and of technological knowledge. A socialist government too would be eager to use the available factors of production for producing those goods that, according to its opinion, are most urgently needed, and to forego the production of those goods which it considers less urgently needed. But the unfeasibility of economic calculation will make it impossible to find out which methods for the production of the goods needed are the most economical ones.

The socialist governments of Russia and Germany are

1. For a more searching treatment of this primordial problem see: Mises, *Socialism, an Economic and Sociological Analysis,* translated by Kahane (New York, 1936), pp. 113–122, 131–142, 516–521; Mises, *Nationaloekonomie* (Geneva, 1940), pp. 188–223, 634–645; Hayek, *Collectivist Economic Planning* (London, 1935); Hayek, "Socialist Calculation: The Competitive Solution" (*Economica,* VII, 125–149).

operating in a world the greater part of which still clings to a market economy. They thus are in a position to use for their economic calculation the prices established abroad. Only because they can refer to these prices are they able to calculate, to keep books and to make plans. It would be quite different if every nation were to adopt socialism. Then there would be no more prices for factors of production and economic calculation would be impossible.[2]

2. PUBLIC ENTERPRISE WITHIN A MARKET ECONOMY

The same is the case with enterprises owned and operated by the government or the municipalities of a country in which the greater part of economic activity is under the management of free enterprise. For them too economic calculation offers no difficulties.

We do not need to ask whether or not it would be feasible to manage such government, state, and municipal enterprises in the same way as private enterprise. For it is a fact that as a rule the authorities are inclined to deviate from the profit system. They do not want to operate their enterprises from the viewpoint of the attainment of the greatest possible profit. They consider the accomplishment of other tasks more important. They are ready to renounce profit or at least a part of profit or even to take a loss for the achievement of other ends.

Whatever these other goals aimed at may be, the result of such a policy always amounts to subsidizing some people to the burden of others. If a government-owned enterprise operates at a loss or with a part only of the profit which it could attain if it were conducted solely according to the profit motive, the falling off affects the budget and thereby the taxpayers. If, for instance, a city-owned transportation system charges the customers so low a fare that the costs of the operation cannot be covered, the taxpayers are virtually subsidizing those riding the trains.

2. Mises, *Omnipotent Government* (New Haven, 1944), pp. 55–58.

But we need not, in a book dealing with the problems of bureaucracy, bother about these financial aspects. From our point of view another outcome is to be considered.

As soon as an undertaking is no longer operated under the profit motive, other principles must be adopted for the conduct of its affairs. The city authorities cannot simply instruct the manager: Do *not* bother about a profit. They must give him more definite and precise orders. What kind of orders could these be?

The champions of nationalized and municipalized enterprise are prone to answer this question in a rather naïve manner: The public enterprise's duty is to render useful services to the community. But the problem is not so simple as this. Every undertaking's sole task is to render useful services. But what does this term mean? Who is, in the case of public enterprise, to decide whether a service is useful? And much more important: How do we find out whether the services rendered are not too heavily paid for, i.e., whether the factors of production absorbed by their performance are not withdrawn from other lines of utilization in which they could render more valuable services?

With private profit-seeking enterprise this problem is solved by the attitudes of the public. The proof of the usefulness of the services rendered is that a sufficient number of citizens is ready to pay the price asked for them. There cannot be any doubt about the fact that the customers consider the services rendered by the bakeries useful. They are ready to pay the price asked for bread. Under this price the production of bread tends to expand until saturation is reached, that is, until a further expansion would withdraw factors of production from branches of industry for whose products the demand of the consumers is more intense. In taking the profit-motive as a guide, free enterprise adjusts its activities to the desires of the public. The profit-motive pushes every entrepreneur to accomplish those services that the consumers deem the most urgent. The price structure of the market tells them how free they are to invest in every branch of production.

But if a public enterprise is to be operated without regard to profits, the behavior of the public no longer provides a criterion of its usefulness. If the government or the municipal authorities are resolved to go on notwithstanding the fact that the operation costs are not made up by the payments received from the customers, where may a criterion be found of the usefulness of the services rendered? How can we find out whether the deficit is not too big with regard to these services? And how discover whether the deficit could not be reduced without impairing the value of the services?

A private business is doomed if its operation brings losses only and no way can be found to remedy this situation. Its unprofitability is the proof of the fact that the consumers disallow it. There is, with private enterprise, no means of defying this verdict of the public and of keeping on. The manager of a plant involving a loss may explain and excuse the failure. But such apologies are of no avail; they cannot prevent the final abandonment of the unsuccessful project.

It is different with a public enterprise. Here the appearance of a deficit is not considered a proof of failure. The manager is not responsible for it. It is the aim of his boss, the government, to sell at such a low price that a loss becomes unavoidable. But if the government were to limit its interference with the fixing of the sales prices and to leave everything else to the manager, it would give him full power to draw on the treasury's funds.

It is important to realize that our problem has nothing at all to do with the necessity of preventing the manager from the criminal abuse of his power. We assume that the government or the municipality has appointed an honest and efficient manager and that the moral climate of the country or city and the organization of the undertaking concerned offer a satisfactory protection against any feloni-

ous misprision. Our problem is quite different. It stems from
the fact that every service can be improved by increasing
expenditures. However excellent a hospital, subway system, or water works may be, the manager always knows
how he could improve the service provided the funds required are available. In no field of human wants can full
satisfaction be reached in such a way that no further improvement is possible. The specialists are intent upon improving the satisfaction of needs only in their special
branches of activity. They do not and cannot bother about
the check which an expansion of the plant entrusted to them
would impose upon other classes of need-satisfaction. It is
not the task of the hospital director to renounce some improvement of the municipal hospital lest it impede the improvement of the subway system or vice versa. It is precisely the efficient and honest manager who will try to make
the services of his outfit as good as possible. But as he is
not restrained by any considerations of financial success, the
costs involved would place a heavy burden on the public
funds. He would become a sort of irresponsible spender of
the taxpayers' money. As this is out of the question, the
government must give attention to many details of the
management. It must define in a precise way the quality
and the quantity of the services to be rendered and the
commodities to be sold, it must issue detailed instructions
concerning the methods to be applied in the purchase of
material factors of production and in hiring and rewarding
labor. As the account of profit or loss is not to be considered
the criterion of the management's success or failure, the
only means to make the manager responsible to the boss,
the treasury, is to limit his discretion by rules and regulations. If he believes that it is expedient to spend more than
these instructions allow, he must make an application for a
special allotment of money. In this case the decision rests
with his boss, the government, or the municipality. At any
rate the manager is not a business executive but a bureaucrat,
that is, an officer bound to abide by various instructions. The

criterion of good management is not the approval of the customers resulting in an excess of revenue over costs but the strict obedience to a set of bureaucratic rules. The supreme rule of management is subservience to such rules.

Of course, the government or the town council will be eager to draft these rules and regulations in such a way that the services rendered become as useful as they want them to be and the deficit not higher than they want to have it. But this does not remove the bureaucratic character of the conduct of affairs. The management is under the necessity of abiding by a code of instructions; this alone matters. The manager is not answerable if his actions are correct from the point of view of this code. His main task cannot be efficiency as such, but efficiency within the limits of subservience to the regulations. His position is not that of an executive in a profit-seeking enterprise but that of a civil servant, for instance, the head of a police department.

The only alternative to profit-seeking business is bureaucratic management. It would be utterly impracticable to delegate to any individual or group of individuals the power to draw freely on public funds. It is necessary to curb the power of the managers of nationalized or municipalized systems by bureaucratic makeshifts if they are not to be made irresponsible spenders of public money and if their management is not to disorganize the whole budget.

IV

BUREAUCRATIC MANAGEMENT OF PRIVATE ENTERPRISES

I. HOW GOVERNMENT INTERFERENCE AND THE IMPAIRMENT OF THE PROFIT MOTIVE DRIVE BUSINESS TOWARD BUREAUCRATIZATION

NO private enterprise will ever fall prey to bureaucratic methods of management if it is operated with the sole aim of making profit. It has already been pointed out that under the profit motive every industrial aggregate, no matter how big it may be, is in a position to organize its whole business and each part of it in such a way that the spirit of capitalist acquisitiveness permeates it from top to bottom.

But ours is an age of a general attack on the profit motive. Public opinion condemns it as highly immoral and extremely detrimental to the commonweal. Political parties and governments are anxious to remove it and to put in its place what they call the "service" point of view and what is in fact bureaucratic management.

We do not need to deal in detail with what the Nazis have achieved in this regard. The Nazis have succeeded in entirely eliminating the profit motive from the conduct of business. In Nazi Germany there is no longer any question of free enterprise. There are no more entrepreneurs. The former entrepreneurs have been reduced to the status of *Betriebsführer* (shop manager). They are not free in their operation; they are bound to obey unconditionally the orders issued by the Central Board of Production Management, the *Reichswirtschaftsministerium*, and its subordinate district and branch offices. The government not only determines the prices and interest rates to be paid and to be asked, the height of wages and salaries, the amount to be produced and the methods to be applied in production; it allots a definite income to every shop manager, thus virtually transforming him into a salaried civil servant. This system has, but for the use of some terms, nothing in common with capitalism and a market economy. It is simply socialism of the German pattern, *Zwangswirtschaft*. It differs from the Russian pattern of socialism, the system of outright nationalization of all plants, only in technical matters. And it is, of course, like the Russian system, a mode of social organization that is purely authoritarian.

In the rest of the world things have not gone as far as that. In the Anglo-Saxon countries there is still private enterprise. But the general tendency of our time is to let the government interfere with private business. And this interference in many instances forces upon the private enterprise bureaucratic management.

2. INTERFERENCE WITH THE HEIGHT OF PROFIT

The government may apply various methods in order to restrict the profits which an enterprise is free to earn. The most frequent methods are:

1. The profits that a special class of undertakings is free to make are limited. A surplus is either to be handed over to the authority (for instance, the city) or to be distributed as a bonus to the employees or it must be eliminated by a reduction of the rates or prices charged to the customers.

2. The authority is free to determine the prices or rates that the enterprise is entitled to charge for the commodities sold or the services rendered. It uses this power for the prevention of what it calls excessive profits.

3. The enterprise is not free to charge more for commodities sold and services rendered than its actual costs plus an additional amount determined by the author-

ity either as a percentage of the costs or as a fixed fee.
4. The enterprise is free to earn as much as market conditions allow; but taxes absorb all profit or the greater
   part of it above a certain amount.

What is common to all these instances is the fact that the
enterprise is no longer interested in increasing its profits.
It loses the incentive to lower costs and to do its job as effi-
ciently and as cheaply as possible. But on the other hand
all the checks on improvements in the procedures and on
attempts to reduce costs remain. The risks connected with
the adoption of new cost saving devices fall upon the entrepreneur. The disagreements involved in resisting the
demand of the employees for higher wages and salaries are
left to him.

Public opinion, biased by the spurious fables of the socialists, is rash in blaming the entrepreneurs. It is, we are
told, their immorality that results in the lowering of efficiency. If they were as conscientious and devoted to the
promotion of public welfare as the unselfish civil servants
are, they would unswervingly aim to the best of their abilities at an improvement in service although their selfish
profit interests are not involved. It is their mean greed that
jeopardizes the working of enterprises under limited profit
chances. Why should a man not do his best even if he may
not expect any personal advantage from the most beneficial
performance of his duties?

Nothing could be more nonsensical than to hold the bureaucrat up in this way as a model for the entrepreneur. The
bureaucrat is not free to aim at improvement. He is bound
to obey rules and regulations established by a superior body.
He has no right to embark upon innovations if his superiors
do not approve of them. His duty and his virtue is to be
obedient.

Let us take as an example the conditions of army life.
Armies are certainly the most ideal and perfect bureaucratic
organizations. In most countries they are commanded by

officers who are sincerely dedicated to one goal only: to make their own nation's armed forces as efficient as possible. Nevertheless the conduct of military affairs is characterized by a stubborn hostility to every attempt toward improvement. It has been said that the general staffs are always preparing for the last war, never for the future war. Every new idea always meets with adamant opposition on the part of those in charge of the management. The champions of progress have had most unpleasant experiences. There is no need to insist upon these facts; they are familiar to everybody.

The reason for this unsatisfactory state of affairs is obvious. Progress of any kind is always at variance with the old and established ideas and therefore with the codes inspired by them. Every step of progress is a change involving heavy risks. Only a few men, endowed with exceptional and rare abilities, have the gift of planning new things and of recognizing their blessings. Under capitalism the innovator is free to embark upon an attempt to realize his plans in spite of the unwillingness of the majority to acknowledge their merits. It is enough if he succeeds in persuading some reasonable men to lend him funds to start with. Under a bureaucratic system it is necessary to convince those at the top, as a rule old men accustomed to do things in prescribed ways, and no longer open to new ideas. No progress and no reforms can be expected in a state of affairs where the first step is to obtain the consent of the old men. The pioneers of new methods are considered rebels and are treated as such. For a bureaucratic mind law abidance, i.e., clinging to the customary and antiquated, is the first of all virtues.

To say to the entrepreneur of an enterprise with limited profit chances, "Behave as the conscientious bureaucrats do," is tantamount to telling him to shun any reform. Nobody can be at the same time a correct bureaucrat and an innovator. Progress is precisely that which the rules and regulations did not foresee; it is necessarily outside the field of bureaucratic activities.

The virtue of the profit system is that it puts on improvements a premium high enough to act as an incentive to take high risks. If this premium is removed or seriously curtailed, there cannot be any question of progress.

Big business spends considerable sums on research because it is eager to profit from new methods of production. Every entrepreneur is always on the search for improvement; he wants to profit either from lowering costs or from perfecting his products. The public sees only the successful innovation. It does not realize how many enterprises failed because they erred in adopting new procedures.

It is vain to ask an entrepreneur to embark, in spite of the absence of a profit incentive, on all the improvements which he would have put to work if the expected profit were to enrich him. The free enterpriser makes his decision on close and careful examination of all the pros and cons and on a weighing of the chances of success and failure. He balances possible gain against possible loss. Either loss or gain will occur in his own fortune. This is essential. Balancing the risk of losing one's own money against the government's or other people's chance for profit means viewing the matter from a quite different angle.

But there is also something much more important. A faulty innovation must not only impair the capital invested, it must no less reduce future profits. The greater part of these profits would have flowed, if earned, into the treasury. Now, their falling off affects the government's revenue. The government will not permit the enterpriser to risk what it considers to be its own revenue. It will think that it is not justified in leaving the enterpriser the right to expose to loss what is virtually the government's money. It will restrict the entrepreneur's freedom to manage his "own" affairs, which practically are no longer his own but the government's.

We are already at the beginning of such policies. In the case of cost-plus contracts the government tries to satisfy itself not only as to whether the costs claimed by the contractor were actually incurred, but no less whether they are allowable under the terms of the contract. It takes every reduction in costs incurred for granted, but it does not acknowledge expenditures which, in the opinion of its employees, the bureaucrats, are not necessary. The resulting situation is this: The contractor spends some money with the intention of reducing costs of production. If he succeeds, the result is—under the cost plus a percentage of cost method—that his profit is curtailed. If he does not succeed, the government does not reimburse the outlays in question and he loses too. Every attempt to change anything in the traditional routine of production has to turn out badly for him. The only way to avoid being penalized is for him not to change anything.

In the field of taxation the limitations placed on salaries are the starting point of a new development. They affect, at present, only the higher salaries. But they will hardly stop here. Once the principle is accepted, that the Bureau of Internal Revenue has the right to declare whether certain costs, deductions, or losses are justified or not, the powers of the enterpriser will also be restricted with regard to other items of costs. Then the management will be under the necessity of assuring itself, before it embarks upon any change, whether the tax authorities approve of the required expenditure. The Collectors of Internal Revenue will become the supreme authorities in matters of manufacturing.

3. INTERFERENCE WITH THE CHOICE OF PERSONNEL

Every kind of government meddling with the business of private enterprise results in the same disastrous consequences. It paralyzes initiative and breeds bureaucratism. We cannot investigate all the methods applied. It will be enough to consider one especially obnoxious instance.

Even in the nineteenth century, in the prime of European liberalism, private enterprise was never so free as it once was in this country. In continental Europe every enterprise and particularly every corporation always depended in many respects on the discretion of government agencies. Bureaus had the power of inflicting serious damage upon every firm. In order to avoid such detriments it was necessary for the management to live on good terms with those in power.

The most frequent procedure was to yield to the government's wishes concerning the composition of the board of directors. Even in Great Britain a board of directors which did not include several peers was considered not quite respectable. In continental Europe and especially in Eastern and Southern Europe the boards were full of former cabinet ministers and generals, of politicians and of cousins, brothers-in-law, schoolmates, and other friends of such dignitaries. With these directors no commercial ability or business experience was required.

The presence of such ignoramuses on the board of directors was by and large innocuous. All they did was to collect their fees and share in the profits. But there were other relatives and friends of those in power who were not eligible for directorships. For them there were salaried positions on the staff. These men were much more a liability than an asset.

With the increasing government interference with business it became necessary to appoint executives whose main duty it was to smooth away difficulties with the authorities. First it was only one vice-president in charge of "affairs referring to government administration." Later the main requirement for the president and for all vice-presidents was to be in good standing with the government and the political parties. Finally no corporation could afford the "luxury" of an executive unpopular with the administration, the labor-unions, and the great political parties. Former government officials, assistant secretaries, and councilors of the various ministries were considered the most appropriate choice for executive positions.

Such executives did not care a whit for the company's prosperity. They were accustomed to bureaucratic management and they accordingly altered the conduct of the corporation's business. Why bother about bringing out better and cheaper products if one can rely on support on the part of the government? For them government contracts, more effective tariff protection, and other government favors were the main concern. And they paid for such privileges by contributions to party funds and government propaganda funds and by appointing people sympathetic to the authorities.

It is long since the staffs of the big German corporations were selected from the viewpoint of commercial and technological ability. Ex-members of smart and politically reliable students' clubs often had a better chance of employment and advancement than efficient experts.

American conditions are very different. As in every sphere of bureaucracy, America is "backward" in the field of bureaucratization of private enterprise also. It is an open question whether Secretary Ickes was right in saying: "Every big business is a bureaucracy." [1] But if the Secretary of the Interior is right, or as far as he is right, this is not an outcome of the evolution of private business but of the growing government interference with business.

4. UNLIMITED DEPENDENCE ON THE DISCRETION OF GOVERNMENT BUREAUS

Every American businessman who has had the opportunity to become acquainted with economic conditions in Southern and Eastern Europe condenses his observations into two points: The entrepreneurs of these countries do not bother about production efficiency, and the governments are in the hands of corrupt cliques. This characterization is by and large correct. But it fails to mention that both

1. *The New York Times Magazine*, January 16, 1944, p. 9.

industrial inefficiency and corruption are the consequences of methods of government interference with business as applied in these countries.

Under this system the government has unlimited power to ruin every enterprise or to lavish favors upon it. The success or failure of every business depends entirely upon the free discretion of those in office. If the businessman does not happen to be a citizen of a powerful foreign nation whose diplomatic and consular agents grant him protection, he is at the mercy of the administration and the ruling party. They can take away all his property and imprison him. On the other hand, they can make him rich.

The government determines the height of tariffs and freight rates. It grants or denies import and export licenses. Every citizen or resident is bound to sell all his proceeds in foreign exchange to the government at a price fixed by the government. On the other hand, the government is the only seller of foreign exchange; it is free to refuse ad libitum applications for foreign exchange. In Europe where almost every kind of production depends upon the importation of equipment, machinery, raw materials, and half-finished goods from abroad, such a refusal is tantamount to a closing of the factory. The final determination of taxes due is practically left to the unlimited discretion of the authorities. The government can use any pretext for the seizure of any plant or shop. Parliament is a puppet in the hands of the rulers; the courts are packed.

In such an environment the entrepreneur must resort to two means: diplomacy and bribery. He must use these methods not only with regard to the ruling party, but no less with regard to the outlawed and persecuted opposition groups which one day may seize the reins. It is a dangerous kind of double-dealing; only men devoid of fear and inhibitions can last in this rotten milieu. Businessmen who have grown up under the conditions of a more liberal age have to leave and are replaced by adventurers. West-European and American entrepreneurs, used to an environment of legality and correctness, are lost unless they secure the services of native agents.

This system, of course, does not offer much incentive for technological improvement. The entrepreneur considers additional investment only if he can buy the machinery on credit from a foreign firm. Being a debtor of a corporation of one of the Western countries is deemed an advantage because one expects that the diplomats concerned will interfere for the protection of the creditor and thus help the debtor too. New branches of production are inaugurated only if the government grants such a premium that huge profits are to be hoped for.

It would be a mistake to place the blame for this corruption on the system of government interference with business and bureaucratism as such. It is bureaucratism degenerated into racketeering in the hands of depraved politicians. Yet we must realize that these countries would have avoided the evil if they had not abandoned the system of free enterprise. Economic postwar reconstruction must start in these countries with a radical change in their policies.

V

THE SOCIAL AND POLITICAL IMPLI-
CATIONS OF BUREAUCRATIZATION

I. THE PHILOSOPHY OF BUREAUCRATISM

THE antagonism which the people had to encounter
in earlier struggles for freedom was simple and
could be understood by everybody. There were
on the one side the tyrants and their supporters; there were
on the other side the advocates of popular government.
The political conflicts were struggles of various groups for
supremacy. The question was: Who should rule? We or
they? The few or the many? The despot or the aristocracy
or the people?

Today the fashionable philosophy of *Statolatry* has ob-
fuscated the issue. The political conflicts are no longer seen
as struggles between groups of men. They are considered
a war between two principles, the good and the bad. The
good is embodied in the great god State, the materializa-
tion of the eternal idea of morality, and the bad in the
"rugged individualism" of selfish men.[1] In this antagonism
the State is always right and the individual always wrong.
The State is the representative of the commonweal, of justice, civilization, and superior wisdom. The individual is
a poor wretch, a vicious fool.

When a German says "der Staat" or when a Marxian
says "society," they are overwhelmed by reverential awe.
How can a man be so entirely corrupt as to rise in rebellion
against this Supreme Being?

Louis XIV was very frank and sincere when he said: I

---

1. Such is the political interpretation of the issue. For the current economic
interpretation see below pp. 117–119.

am the State. The modern etatist is modest. He says: I am
the servant of the State; but, he implies, the State is God.
You could revolt against a Bourbon king, and the French
did it. This was, of course, a struggle of man against man.
But you cannot revolt against the god State and against his
humble handy man, the bureaucrat.

Let us not question the sincerity of the well-intentioned
officeholder. He is fully imbued with the idea that it is his
sacred duty to fight for his idol against the selfishness of
the populace. He is, in his opinion, the champion of the
eternal divine law. He does not feel himself *morally* bound
by the human laws which the defenders of individualism
have written into the statutes. Men cannot alter the genuine
laws of god, the State. The individual citizen, in violating
one of the laws of his country, is a criminal deserving punishment. He has acted for his own selfish advantage. But
it is quite a different thing if an officeholder evades the
duly promulgated laws of the nation for the benefit of the
"State." In the opinion of "reactionary" courts he may be
technically guilty of a contravention. But in a higher moral
sense he was right. He has broken human laws lest he
violate a divine law.

This is the essence of the philosophy of bureaucratism.
The written laws are in the eyes of the officials barriers
erected for the protection of scoundrels against the fair
claims of society. Why should a criminal evade punishment
only because the "State" in prosecuting him has violated
some frivolous formalities? Why should a man pay lower
taxes only because there is a loophole left in the tax law?
Why should lawyers make a living advising people how to
profit from the imperfections of the written law? What is
the use of all these restrictions imposed by the written law
upon the government official's honest endeavors to make
the people happy? If only there were no constitutions, bills
of rights, laws, parliaments, and courts! No newspapers
and no attorneys! How fine the world would be if the
"State" were free to cure all ills!

It is one step only from such a mentality to the perfect totalitarianism of Stalin and Hitler.

The answer to be given to these bureaucratic radicals is obvious. The citizen may reply: You may be excellent and lofty men, much better than we other citizens are. We do not question your competence and your intelligence. But you are not the vicars of a god called "the State." You are servants of the law, the duly passed laws of our nation. It is not your business to criticize the law, still less to violate it. In violating the law you are perhaps worse than a good many of the racketeers, no matter how good your intentions may be. For you are appointed, sworn, and paid to enforce the law, not to break it. The worst law is better than bureaucratic tyranny.

The main difference between a policeman and a kidnaper and between a tax collector and a robber is that the policeman and the tax collector obey and enforce the law, while the kidnaper and robber violate it. Remove the law, and society will be destroyed by anarchy. The State is the only institution entitled to apply coercion and compulsion and to inflict harm upon individuals. This tremendous power cannot be abandoned to the discretion of some men, however competent and clever they may deem themselves. It is necessary to restrict its application. This is the task of the laws.

The officeholders and the bureaucrats are not the State. They are men selected for the application of the laws. One may call such opinions orthodox and doctrinaire. They are indeed the expression of old wisdom. But the alternative to the rule of law is the rule of despots.

2. BUREAUCRATIC COMPLACENCY

The officeholder's task is to serve the public. His office has been established—directly or indirectly—by a legislative act and by the allocation of the means necessary for its support in the budget. He executes the laws of his country.

In performing his duties he shows himself a useful member of the community, even if the laws which he has to put into practice are detrimental to the commonweal. For it is not he who is responsible for their inadequacy. The sovereign people is to blame, not the faithful executor of the people's will. As the distillers are not responsible for people getting drunk, so the government's clerks are not responsible for the undesirable consequences of unwise laws.

On the other hand, it is not the merit of the bureaucrats that many benefits are derived from their actions. That the police department's work is so efficient that the citizens are fairly well protected against murder, robbery, and theft does not oblige the rest of the people to be more grateful to the police officers than to any other fellow citizens rendering useful services. The police officer and the fireman have no better claim to the public's gratitude than the doctors, the railroad engineers, the welders, the sailors, or the manufacturers of any useful commodity. The traffic cop has no more cause for conceit than the manufacturer of traffic lights. It is not his merit that his superiors assigned him to a duty in which he daily and hourly prevents accidental killing and thus saves many people's lives.

It is true that society could not do without the services rendered by patrolmen, tax collectors, and clerks of the courts. But it is no less true that everyone would suffer great damage if there were no scavengers, chimney sweepers, dishwashers, and bug exterminators. Within the framework of social coöperation every citizen depends on the services rendered by all his fellow citizens. The great surgeon and the eminent musician would never have been able to concentrate all their efforts upon surgery and music if the division of labor had not freed them from the necessity of taking care of many trifles the performance of which would have prevented them from becoming perfect specialists. The ambassador and the lighthousekeeper have no better claim to the epithet *pillar of society* than the Pullman porter and the charwoman. For, under the division of labor,

the structure of society rests on the shoulders of all men
and women.

There are, of course, men and women serving in an
altruistic and entirely detached way. Mankind would never
have reached the present state of civilization without hero-
ism and self-sacrifice on the part of an elite. Every step
forward on the way toward an improvement of moral conditions has been an achievement of men who were ready to
sacrifice their own well-being, their health, and their lives
for the sake of a cause that they considered just and beneficial. They did what they considered their duty without
bothering whether they themselves would not be victim-
ized. These people did not work for the sake of reward,
they served their cause unto death.

It was a purposeful confusion on the part of the German
metaphysicians of statolatry that they clothed all men in
the government service with the gloriole of such altruistic
self-sacrifice. From the writings of the German etatists the
civil servant emerges as a saintly being, a sort of monk who
forsook all earthly pleasures and all personal happiness
in order to serve, to the best of his abilities, God's lieutenant,
once the Hohenzollern king and today the Führer. The
Staatsbeamte does not work for pay because no salary however large could be considered an adequate reward for
the invaluable and priceless benefits that society derives
from his self-denying sacrifice. Society owes him not pay
but a maintenance adequate to his rank in the official hierarchy. It is a misnomer to call this maintenance a salary.[2]
Only liberals, biased by the prejudices and errors of com-
mercialism, use such a wrong term. If the *Beamtengehalt*
(the civil servant's salary) were a real salary, it would be
only just and natural to give the holder of the most modest
office an income higher than that of anybody outside of the
official hierarchy. Every civil servant is, when on duty, a
mandatory of the State's sovereignty and infallibility. His

2. Cf. Laband, *Das Staatsrecht des Deutschen Reiches* (5th ed. Tübingen,
1911), I, 500.

testimony in court counts more than that of the layman.

All this was sheer nonsense. In all countries most people joined the staff of the government offices because the salary and the pension offered were higher than what they could expect to earn in other occupations. They did not renounce anything in serving the government. Civil service was for them the most profitable job they could find.

The incentive offered by the civil service in Europe consisted not only in the level of the salary and the pension; many applicants, and not the best ones, were attracted by the ease of the work and by the security. As a rule government jobs were less exigent than those in business. Besides, the appointments were for life. An employee could be dismissed only when a kind of judicial trial had found him guilty of heinous neglect of his duties. In Germany, Russia, and France, every year many thousands of boys whose life plan was completely fixed entered the lowest grade of the system of secondary education. They would take their degrees, they would get a job in one of the many departments, they would serve thirty or forty years, and then retire with a pension. Life had no surprises and no sensations for them, everything was plain and known beforehand.

The difference between the social prestige of government jobs in continental Europe and in America may be illustrated by an example. In Europe social and political discrimination against a minority group took the form of barring such people from access to all government jobs, no matter how modest the position and the salary. In Germany, in the Austro-Hungarian Empire, and in many other countries all those subordinate jobs that did not require special abilities or training—like attendants, ushers, heralds, beadles, apparitors, messengers, janitors—were legally reserved for ex-soldiers who had voluntarily given more years of active service in the armed forces than the minimum required by the law. These jobs were considered highly valued rewards for noncommissioned officers. In the eyes of the people, it was a privilege to serve as an attendant in a bureau. If in Germany there had been a class of the social status of the American Negro, such persons would never have ventured to apply for one of these jobs. They would have known that such an ambition was extravagant for them.

3. THE BUREAUCRAT AS A VOTER

The bureaucrat is not only a government employee. He is, under a democratic constitution, at the same time a voter and as such a part of the sovereign, his employer. He is in a peculiar position: he is both employer and employee. And his pecuniary interest as employee towers above his interest as employer, as he gets much more from the public funds than he contributes to them.

This double relationship becomes more important as the people on the government's pay roll increase. The bureaucrat as voter is more eager to get a raise than to keep the budget balanced. His main concern is to swell the pay roll.

The political structure of Germany and France, in the last years preceding the fall of their democratic constitutions, was to a very great extent influenced by the fact that for a considerable part of the electorate the state was the source of income. There were not only the hosts of public employees, and those employed in the nationalized branches of business (e.g., railroad, post, telegraph, and telephone), there were the receivers of the unemployment dole and of social security benefits, as well as the farmers and some other groups which the government directly or indirectly subsidized. Their main concern was to get more out of the public funds. They did not care for "ideal" issues like liberty, justice, the supremacy of the law, and good government. They asked for more money, that was all. No candidate for parliament, provincial diets, or town councils could risk opposing the appetite of the public employees for a raise. The various political parties were eager to outdo one another in munificence.

In the nineteenth century the parliaments were intent on restricting public expenditures as much as possible. But now thrift became despicable. Boundless spending was considered a wise policy. Both the party in power and the opposition strove for popularity by openhandedness. To create new offices with new employees was called a "positive" policy, and every attempt to prevent squandering public funds was disparaged as "negativism."

Representative democracy cannot subsist if a great part of the voters are on the government pay roll. If the members of parliament no longer consider themselves mandatories of the taxpayers but deputies of those receiving salaries, wages, subsidies, doles, and other benefits from the treasury, democracy is done for.

This is one of the antinomies inherent in present-day constitutional issues. It has made many people despair of the future of democracy. As they became convinced that the trend toward more government interference with business, toward more offices with more employees, toward more doles and subsidies is inevitable, they could not help losing confidence in government by the people.

4. THE BUREAUCRATIZATION OF THE MIND

The modern trend toward government omnipotence and totalitarianism would have been nipped in the bud if its advocates had not succeeded in indoctrinating youth with their tenets and in preventing them from becoming acquainted with the teachings of economics.

Economics is a theoretical science and as such does not tell man what values he should prefer and what ends he should aim at. It does not establish ultimate ends. This is not the task of the thinking man but that of the acting man. Science is a product of thought, action a product of will. In this sense we may say that economics as a science is neutral with regard to the ultimate ends of human endeavor.

But it is different with regard to the means to be applied

for the attainment of given social ends. There economics
is the only reliable guide of action. If men are eager to
succeed in the pursuit of any social ends, they must adjust
their conduct to the results of economic thinking.

The outstanding fact of the intellectual history of the last
hundred years is the struggle against economics. The advocates of government omnipotence did not enter into a discussion of the problems involved. They called the economists names, they cast suspicion upon their motives, they
ridiculed them and called down curses upon them.

It is, however, not the task of this book to deal with this
phenomenon. We have to limit ourselves to the description
of the role that bureaucracy played in this development.

In most countries of the European continent the universities are owned and operated by the government. They
are subject to the control of the Ministry of Education as
a police station is subject to the head of the police department. The teachers are civil servants like patrolmen and
customs officers. Nineteenth-century liberalism tried to
limit the right of the Ministry of Education to interfere
with the freedom of university professors to teach what
they considered true and correct. But as the government
appointed the professors, it appointed only trustworthy and
reliable men, that is, men who shared the government's
viewpoint and were ready to disparage economics and to
teach the doctrine of government omnipotence.

As in all other fields of bureaucratization, nineteenth-
century Germany was far ahead of other nations in this
matter too. Nothing characterizes the spirit of the German
universities better than a passage of an oration that the
physiologist Emil du Bois-Reymond delivered in 1870 in
his double capacity as Rector of the University of Berlin
and as President of the Prussian Academy of Science: "We,
the University of Berlin, quartered opposite the King's
palace, are, by the deed of our foundation, the intellectual
bodyguard of the House of Hohenzollern." The idea that
such a royal henchman should profess views contrary to the

tenets of the government, his employer, was incomprehensible to the Prussian mind. To maintain the theory that there are such things as economic laws was deemed a kind of rebellion. For if there are economic laws, then governments cannot be regarded as omnipotent, as their policies could only succeed when adjusted to the operation of these laws. Thus the main concern of the German professors of the social sciences was to denounce the scandalous heresy that there is a regularity in economic phenomena. The teaching of economics was anathematized and *wirtschaftliche Staatswissenschaften* (economic aspects of political science) put in its place. The only qualities required in an academic teacher of the social sciences were disparagement of the operation of the market system and enthusiastic support of government control. Under the Kaiser radical Marxians who openly advocated a revolutionary upheaval and the violent overthrow of the government were not appointed to full-time professorships; the Weimar Republic virtually abolished this discrimination.

Economics deals with the operation of the whole system of social coöperation, with the interplay of all its determinants, and with the interdependence of the various branches of production. It cannot be broken up into separate fields open to treatment by specialists who neglect the rest. It is simply nonsensical to study money or labor or foreign trade with the same kind of specialization which historians apply when dividing human history into various compartments. The history of Sweden can be treated with almost no reference to the history of Peru. But you cannot deal with wage rates without dealing at the same time with commodity prices, interest rates, and profits. Every change occurring in one of the economic elements affects all other elements. One will never discover what a definite policy or change brings about if one limits his investigation to a special segment of the whole system.

It is precisely this interdependence that the government does not want to see when it meddles in economic affairs.

The government pretends to be endowed with the mystical power to accord favors out of an inexhaustible horn of plenty. It is both omniscient and omnipotent. It can by a magic wand create happiness and abundance.

The truth is that the government cannot give if it does not take from somebody. A subsidy is never paid by the government out of its own funds; it is at the expense of the taxpayer that the state grants subsidies. Inflation and credit expansion, the preferred methods of present-day government openhandedness, do not add anything to the amount of resources available. They make some people more prosperous, but only to the extent that they make others poorer. Interference with the market, with commodity prices, wage rates, and interest rates as determined by demand and supply, may in the short run attain the ends aimed at by the government. But in the long run such measures always result in a state of affairs which—from the viewpoint of the government—is more unsatisfactory than the previous state they were intended to alter.

It is not in the power of the government to make everybody more prosperous. It can raise the income of the farmers by forcibly restricting domestic agricultural production. But the higher prices of farm products are paid by the consumers, not by the state. The counterpart of the farmers' higher standard of living is the lowering of the standard of living of the rest of the nation. The government can protect the small shops against the competition of department stores and chain stores. But here again the consumers foot the bill. The state can improve the conditions of a part of the wage earners by allegedly pro-labor legislation or by giving a free hand to labor-union pressure and compulsion. But if this policy does not result in a corresponding rise in the prices of manufactures, thereby bringing *real* wage rates back to the market level, it brings about unemployment of a considerable part of those willing to earn wages.

A scrutiny of such policies from the viewpoint of economic theory must necessarily show their futility. This is why economics is tabooed by the bureaucrats. But the governments encourage the specialists who limit their observations to a narrow field without bothering about the further consequences of a policy. The labor economist deals only with the immediate results of pro-labor policies, the farm economist only with the rise of agricultural prices. They both view the problems only from the angle of those pressure groups which are immediately favored by the measure in question and disregard its ultimate social consequences. They are not economists, but expounders of government activities in a particular branch of the administration.

For under government interference with business the unity of government policies has long since disintegrated into badly coördinated parts. Gone are the days when it was still possible to speak of a government's policy. Today in most countries each department follows its own course, working against the endeavors of the other departments. The department of labor aims at higher wage rates and at lower living costs. But the same administration's department of agriculture aims at higher food prices, and the department of commerce tries to raise domestic commodity prices by tariffs. One department fights against monopoly, but other departments are eager to bring about—by tariffs, patents, and other means—the conditions required for the building of monopolistic restraint. And each department refers to the expert opinion of those specialized in their respective fields.

Thus the students no longer receive an initiation into economics. They learn incoherent and disconnected facts about various government measures thwarting one another. Their doctor's theses and their graduate research work deal not with economics but with various topics of economic history and various instances of government interference with business. Such detailed and well-documented statistical studies of the conditions of the immediate past (mistakenly often labeled studies about "present-day" conditions) are

of great value for the future historian. They are no less
important for the vocational tasks of lawyers and office
clerks. But they are certainly not a substitute for the lack
of instruction in economics. It is amazing that Stresemann's
doctoral thesis dealt with the conditions of the bottled-beer
trade in Berlin. Under the conditions of the German university curriculum this meant that he devoted a considerable part of his university work to the study of the marketing of beer and of the drinking habits of the population.
This was the intellectual equipment that the glorified German university system gave to a man who later acted as
the Reich's chancellor in the most critical years of German
history.

After the old professors who had got their chairs in the
short flowering of German liberalism had died, it became
impossible to hear anything about economics at the universities of the Reich. There were no longer any German
economists, and the books of foreign economists could not
be found in the libraries of the university seminars. The
social scientists did not follow the example of the professors
of theology who acquainted their students with the tenets
and dogmas of other churches and sects and with the
philosophy of atheism because they were eager to refute
the creeds they deemed heretical. All that the students of
the social sciences learned from their teachers was that economics is a spurious science and that the so-called economists are, as Marx said, sycophantic apologists of the unfair
class interests of bourgeois exploiters, ready to sell the people to big business and finance capital.[3] The graduates left
the universities convinced advocates of totalitarianism
either of the Nazi variety or of the Marxian brand.

Conditions in other countries were similar. The most
eminent establishment of French learning was the *Ecole
Normale Supérieure* in Paris; its graduates filled the most
important posts in public administration, politics and higher

3. Cf. Pohle, *Die gegenwärtige Krise der deutschen Volkswirtschafts-
lehre* (2d ed. Leipzig, 1921).

education. This school was dominated by Marxians and other supporters of full government control. In Russia the Imperial Government did not admit to a university chair anybody suspected of the liberal ideas of "Western" economics. But, on the other hand, it appointed many Marxians of the "loyal" wing of Marxism, i.e., those who kept out of the way of the revolutionary fanatics. Thus the Czars themselves contributed to the later triumph of Marxism.

European totalitarianism is an upshot of bureaucracy's preëminence in the field of education. The universities paved the way for the dictators.

Today both in Russia and in Germany the universities are the main strongholds of the one-party system. Not only the social sciences, history, and philosophy, but all other branches of knowledge, of art, and of literature are regimented or, as the Nazis say, *gleichgeschaltet*. Even Sidney and Beatrice Webb, naïve and uncritical admirers of the Soviets as they are, were shocked when they discovered that the *Journal for Marxist-Leninist Natural Sciences* stands "for party in mathematics" and "for the purity of Marxist-Leninist theory in surgery" and that the *Soviet Herald of Venereology and Dermatology* aims at considering all problems that it discusses from the point of view of dialectical materialism.[4]

5. WHO SHOULD BE THE MASTER?

Under any system of the division of labor a principle for the coördination of the activities of the various specialists is needed. The specialist's effort would be aimless and contrary to purpose if he were not to find a guide in the supremacy of the public. Of course, production's only end is to serve the consumers.

Under a market society the profit motive is the directing principle. Under government control it is regimentation.

4. Sidney and Beatrice Webb, *Soviet Communism: A New Civilization?* (New York, 1936), II, 1000.

There is no third possibility left. To a man not driven by the impulse to make money on the market some code must say what to do and how.

One of the most frequent objections raised against the liberal and democratic system of capitalism is that it stresses mainly the individual's rights, to the neglect of his duties. People stand on their rights and forget their obligations. However, from the social viewpoint the duties of the citizens are more important than their rights.

There is no need for us to dwell upon the political and constitutional aspect of this antidemocratic critique. The rights of man as codified in the various bills of rights are promulgated for the protection of the individual against governmental arbitrariness. But for them all people would be slaves of despotic rulers.

In the economic sphere the right to acquire and to own property is not a privilege. It is the principle that safeguards the best satisfaction of the wants of the consumers. He who is eager to earn, to acquire, and to hold wealth is under the necessity of serving the consumers. The profit motive is the means of making the public supreme. The better a man succeeds in supplying the consumers, the greater become his earnings. It is to everybody's advantage that the entrepreneur who produces good shoes at the cheapest cost becomes rich; most people would suffer some loss if a law were to limit his right to get richer. Such a law would only favor his less efficient competitors. It would not lower but raise the price of shoes.

Profit is the reward for the best fulfillment of some voluntarily assumed duties. It is the instrument that makes the masses supreme. The common man is the customer for whom the captains of industry and all their aides are working.

It has been objected that this is not true as far as big business is concerned. The consumer has no other choice than either to patronize the business or to forego the satisfaction of a vital need. He is thus forced to submit to any price asked by the entrepreneur. Big business is no longer a supplier and purveyor but a master. It is not under the necessity of improving and cheapening its service.

Let us consider the case of a railroad connecting two cities not connected by any other rail line. We may even ignore the fact that other means of transportation are in competition with the railroad: busses, passenger cars, aeroplanes, and river boats. Under these assumptions it is true that whoever wants to travel is forced to patronize the railroad. But this does not remove the company's interest in good and cheap service. Not all those who consider traveling are forced to make the journey under any conditions. The number of passengers both for pleasure and for business depends on the efficiency of the service and on the rates charged. Some people will travel in any case. Others will travel only if the quality and speed of the service and cheap rates make traveling attractive. It is precisely this second group whose patronage means for the company the difference between dull or even bad business and profitable business. If this is true for a railroad under the extreme assumptions made above, it is much more true for any other branch of business.

All specialists, whether businessmen or professional people, are fully aware of their dependence on the consumers' directives. Daily experience teaches them that, under capitalism, their main task is to serve the consumers. Those specialists who lack an understanding of the fundamental social problems resent very deeply this "servitude" and want to be freed. The revolt of narrow-minded experts is one of the powerful forces pushing toward general bureaucratization.

The architect must adjust his blueprints to the wishes of those for whom he builds homes; or—in the case of apartment houses—of the proprietors who want to own a building that suits the tastes of the prospective tenants and can therefore be easily rented. There is no need to find out whether the architect is right in believing that he knows better what a fine house should look like than the foolish laymen who lack good taste. He may foam with rage when he is forced to debase his wonderful projects in order to please his customers. And he yearns for an ideal state of affairs in which he could build homes that meet his own artistic standards. He longs for a government housing office and sees himself in his daydreams at the top of this bureau. Then he will construct dwellings according to his own fashion.

This architect would be highly offended if somebody were to call him a would-be dictator. My only aim, he could retort, is to make people happy by providing them with finer houses; these people are too ignorant to know what would best promote their own well-being; the expert, under the auspices of the government, must take care of them; there should be a law against ugly buildings. But, let us ask, who is to decide which kind of architectural style has to be considered good and which bad? Our architect will answer: Of course, I, the expert. He boldly disregards the fact that there is, even among the architects, very considerable dissent with regard to styles and artistic values.

We do not want to stress the point that this architect, even under a bureaucratic dictatorship and precisely under such a totalitarianism, will not be free to build according to his own ideas. He will have to comply with the tastes of his bureaucratic superiors, and they themselves will be subject to the whims of the supreme dictator. In Nazi Germany the architects are not free either. They have to accommodate themselves to the plans of the frustrated artist Hitler.

Still more important is this. There are, in the field of esthetics as in all other fields of human endeavor, no absolute criteria of what is beautiful and what is not. If a man *forces* his fellow citizens to submit to his own standards of value, he does not make them any happier. They themselves alone can decide what makes them happy and what they like. You do not increase the happiness of a man eager to attend a performance of *Abie's Irish Rose* by forcing him to attend a perfect performance of *Hamlet* instead. You may deride his poor taste. But he alone is supreme in matters of his own satisfaction.

The dictatorial nutrition expert wants to feed his fellow citizens according to his own ideas about perfect alimentation. He wants to deal with men as the cattle breeder deals with his cows. He fails to realize that nutrition is not an end in itself but the means for the attainment of other ends. The farmer does not feed his cow in order to make it happy but in order to attain some end which the well-fed cow should serve. There are various schemes for feeding cows. Which one of them he chooses depends on whether he wants to get as much milk as possible or as much meat as possible or something else. Every dictator plans to rear, raise, feed, and train his fellow men as the breeder does his cattle. His aim is not to make the people happy but to bring them into a condition which renders him, the dictator, happy. He wants to domesticate them, to give them cattle status. The cattle breeder also is a benevolent despot.

The question is: Who should be the master? Should man be free to choose his own road toward what he thinks will make him happy? Or should a dictator use his fellow men as pawns in his endeavors to make himself, the dictator, happier?

We may admit that some experts are right in telling us that most people behave foolishly in their pursuit of happiness. But you cannot make a man happier by putting him under guardianship. The experts of the various government agencies are certainly fine men. But they are not right in becoming indignant whenever the legislature frustrates their carefully elaborated designs. What is the use of representative government, they ask; it merely thwarts our good intentions. But the only question is: Who should run the country? The voters or the bureaucrats?

Every half-wit can use a whip and force other people to obey. But it requires brains and diligence to serve the public. Only a few people succeed in producing shoes better and cheaper than their competitors. The inefficient expert will always aim at bureaucratic supremacy. He is fully aware of the fact that he cannot succeed within a competitive system. For him all-round bureaucratization is a refuge. Equipped with the power of an office he will enforce his rulings with the aid of the police.

At the bottom of all this fanatical advocacy of planning and socialism there is often nothing else than the intimate consciousness of one's own inferiority and inefficiency. The man who is aware of his inability to stand competition scorns "this mad competitive system." He who is unfit to serve his fellow citizens wants to rule them.

VI

THE PSYCHOLOGICAL CONSE-
QUENCES OF BUREAUCRATIZATION

I. THE GERMAN YOUTH MOVEMENT

HIGH-BROWS turn up their noses at Horatio Alger's philosophy. Yet Alger succeeded better than anybody else in stressing the most characteristic point of capitalist society. Capitalism is a system under which everybody has the chance of acquiring wealth; it gives everybody unlimited opportunity. Not everybody, of course, is favored by good luck. Very few become millionaires. But everybody knows that strenuous effort and nothing less than strenuous effort pays. All roads are open to the smart youngster. He is optimistic in the awareness of his own strength. He has self-confidence and is full of hope. And as he grows older and realizes that many of his plans have been frustrated, he has no cause for despair. His children will start the race again and he does not see any reason why they should not succeed where he himself failed. Life is worth living because it is full of promise.

All this was literally true of America. In old Europe there still survived many checks inherited from the *ancien régime*. Even in the prime of liberalism, aristocracy and officialdom were struggling for the maintenance of their privileges. But in America there were no such remnants of the Dark Ages. It was in this sense a young country, and it was a free country. Here were neither industrial codes nor guilds. Thomas Alva Edison and Henry Ford did not have to overcome any obstacles erected by shortsighted governments and a narrow-minded public opinion.

Under such conditions the rising generation are driven by the spirit of the pioneer. They are born into a progressing society, and they realize that it is their task to contribute something to the improvement of human affairs. They will change the world, shape it according to their own ideas. They have no time to waste, tomorrow is theirs and they must prepare for the great things that are waiting for them. They do not talk about their being young and about the rights of youth; they act as young people must act. They do not boast about their own "dynamism"; they are dynamic and there is no need for them to emphasize this quality. They do not challenge the older generation with arrogant talk. They want to beat it by their deeds.

But it is quite a different thing under the rising tide of bureaucratization. Government jobs offer no opportunity for the display of personal talents and gifts. Regimentation spells the doom of initiative. The young man has no illusions about his future. He knows what is in store for him. He will get a job with one of the innumerable bureaus, he will be but a cog in a huge machine the working of which is more or less mechanical. The routine of a bureaucratic technique will cripple his mind and tie his hands. He will enjoy security. But this security will be rather of the kind that the convict enjoys within the prison walls. He will never be free to make decisions and to shape his own fate. He will forever be a man taken care of by other people. He will never be a real man relying on his own strength. He shudders at the sight of the huge office buildings in which he will bury himself.

In the decade preceding the First World War Germany, the country most advanced on the path toward bureaucratic regimentation, witnessed the appearance of a phenomenon hitherto unheard of: the youth movement. Turbulent gangs of untidy boys and girls roamed the country, making much noise and shirking their school lessons. In bombastic words they announced the gospel of a golden age. All preceding generations, they emphasized, were simply idiotic; their incapacity has converted the earth into a hell. But the rising generation is no longer willing to endure *gerontocracy*, the supremacy of impotent and imbecile senility. Henceforth the brilliant youths will rule. They will destroy everything that is old and useless, they will reject all that was dear to their parents, they will substitute new real and substantial values and ideologies for the antiquated and false ones of capitalist and bourgeois civilization, and they will build a new society of giants and supermen.

The inflated verbiage of these adolescents was only a poor disguise for their lack of any ideas and of any definite program. They had nothing to say but this: We are young and therefore chosen; we are ingenious because we are young; we are the carriers of the future; we are the deadly foes of the rotten bourgeois and Philistines. And if somebody was not afraid to ask them what their plans were, they knew only one answer: Our leaders will solve all problems.

It has always been the task of the new generation to provoke changes. But the characteristic feature of the youth movement was that they had neither new ideas nor plans. They called their action the youth movement precisely because they lacked any program which they could use to give a name to their endeavors. In fact they espoused entirely the program of their parents. They did not oppose the trend toward government omnipotence and bureaucratization. Their revolutionary radicalism was nothing but the impudence of the years between boyhood and manhood; it was a phenomenon of a protracted puberty. It was void of any ideological content.

The chiefs of the youth movement were mentally unbalanced neurotics. Many of them were affected by a morbid sexuality, they were either profligate or homosexual. None of them excelled in any field of activity or contributed anything to human progress. Their names are long since forgotten; the only trace they left were some books and poems preaching sexual perversity. But the bulk of their followers were quite different. They had one aim only: to get a job as soon as possible with the government. Those who were not killed in the wars and revolutions are today pedantic and timid bureaucrats in the innumerable offices of the German *Zwangswirtschaft*. They are obedient and faithful slaves of Hitler. But they will be no less obedient and faithful handy men of Hitler's successor, whether he is a German nationalist or a puppet of Stalin.

From Germany the youth movement spread to other countries. Italian Fascism masked itself as a youth movement. Its party song, "Giovinezza," is a hymn of youth. Its buffoon Duce boasted still in his late fifties of his youthful vigor and was anxious to conceal his age like a coquettish lady. But the only concern of the rank-and-file Fascist was to get a government job. In the time of the Ethiopian war the present writer asked some graduate students of one of the great Italian universities for an explanation of their hostility to France and Great Britain. The answer was amazing: "Italy," they said, "does not offer enough opportunity for its intelligentsia. We want to conquer British and French colonies in order to get in the administration of these territories the jobs which are now in the hands of British and French bureaucrats."

The youth movement was an expression of the uneasiness that young people felt in face of the gloomy prospects that the general trend toward regimentation offered them. But it was a counterfeit rebellion doomed to failure because it did not dare to fight seriously against the growing menace of government all-round control and totalitarianism. The tumultuous would-be rioters were impotent because they were under the spell of the totalitarian superstitions. They indulged in seditious babble and chanted inflammatory songs, but they wanted first of all government jobs.

Today the youth movement is dead in the countries most advanced on the way toward totalitarianism. In Russia, in Germany, and in Italy the children and the adolescents are firmly integrated into the all-embracing apparatus of state control. Children from the tenderest age are members of the political organizations. From the cradle to the grave all citizens are subject to the machine of the one-party system, bound to obey without asking questions. No "private" associations or gatherings are permitted. The official apparatus does not tolerate any competition. The official ideology does not tolerate any dissenters. Such is the reality of the bureaucratic utopia.

2. THE FATE OF THE RISING GENERATION WITHIN A BUREAUCRATIC ENVIRONMENT

The youth movement was an impotent and abortive revolt of youth against the menace of bureaucratization. It was doomed because it did not attack the seed of the evil, the trend toward socialization. It was in fact nothing but a confused expression of uneasiness, without any clear ideas and definite plans. The revolting adolescents were so completely under the spell of socialist ideas that they simply did not know what they wanted.

It is evident that youth is the first victim of the trend toward bureaucratization. The young men are deprived of any opportunity to shape their own fate. For them there is no chance left. They are in fact "lost generations" for they lack the most precious right of every rising generation, the right to contribute something new to the old inventory of civilization. The slogan: *Mankind has reached the stage of maturity*, is their undoing. What are young people to whom nothing is left to change and to improve? Whose only prospect is to start at the lowest rung of the bureaucratic ladder and to climb slowly in strict observance of the rules formulated by older superiors? Seen from their viewpoint bureaucratization means subjection of the young to the domination of the old. This amounts to a return to a sort of caste system.

Among all nations and civilizations—in the ages preceding the rise of modern liberalism and its offspring, capitalism—society was based on status. The nation was divided into castes. There were privileged castes such as kings and noblemen, and underprivileged castes such as serfs and slaves. A man was born into a definite caste, remained in it throughout his whole life and bequeathed his caste status to his children. He who was born into one of the lower castes was forever deprived of the right to attain one of the stations of life reserved to the privileged. Liberalism and capitalism abolished all such discrimination and made all people equal under the law. Now virtually everybody was free to compete for every place in the community.

Marxism provides a different interpretation of liberalism's achievements. The main dogma of Karl Marx is the doctrine of the irreconcilable conflict of economic classes. Capitalist society is divided into classes the interests of which are antagonistic. Thus the class struggle is inevitable. It will disappear only in the future classless society of socialism.

The most remarkable fact about this doctrine is that it has never been explicitly expounded. In the *Communist Manifesto* the instances used for the exemplification of class struggles are taken from the conflict between castes. Then Marx adds that the modern bourgeois society has established new classes. But he never said what a class is and what he had in mind in speaking of classes and class antagonisms and in coördinating classes to castes. All his writings center around these never-defined terms. Although indefatigable in publishing books and articles full of sophisticated definitions and scholastic hairsplitting, Marx never attempted to explain in unambiguous language what the characteristic mark of an economic class is. When he died, thirty-five years after the publication of the *Communist Manifesto*, he left the manuscript of the third volume of his main treatise, *Capital*, unfinished. And, very significantly, the manuscript breaks off just at the point at which the explanation of this fundamental notion of his entire philosophy was to be given. Neither Marx nor any one of the host of Marxian writers could tell us what a social class is, much less whether such social classes really play in the social structure the role assigned to them in the doctrine.

Of course, from the logical viewpoint it is permissible to classify things according to any trait chosen. The question is only whether a classification on the ground of the traits selected is useful for further investigation and for the clarification and amplification of our knowledge. The question is therefore not whether the Marxian classes really exist, but whether they really have the importance attached to them by Marx. Marx failed to provide a precise definition of the concept *social class* that he had used in all his writings in a loose and uncertain way, because a clear definition would have unmasked its futility and its valuelessness for dealing with economic and social problems and the absurdity of coördinating it to social castes.

The characteristic feature of a caste is its rigidity. The social classes, as Marx exemplified them in calling the capitalists, the entrepreneurs, and the wage earners distinct classes, are characterized by their flexibility. There is a perpetual change in the composition of the various classes. Where today are the scions of those who in the days of Marx were entrepreneurs? And where were the ancestors of the contemporary entrepreneurs in the days of Marx? Access to the various stations of modern capitalist society is open to everyone. We may call the United States senators a class without violating logical principles. But it would be a mistake to coördinate them to a hereditary aristocratic caste, notwithstanding the fact that some senators may be descendants of senators of earlier days.

The point has already been stressed that the anonymous forces operating on the market are continuously determining anew who should be entrepreneur and who should be capitalist. The consumers vote, as it were, for those who are to occupy the exalted positions in the setting of the nation's economic structure.

Now under socialism there are neither entrepreneurs nor capitalists. In this sense, namely, that what Marx called a *class* will no longer exist, he was right to call socialism a classless society. But this is of no avail. There will be other differences in social functions which we can call classes with surely no less justification than that of Marx. There will be those who issue orders and those who are bound to obey these orders unconditionally; there will be those who make plans and those whose job it is to execute these plans.

The only thing that counts is the fact that under capitalism everybody is the architect of his own fortune. A boy eager to improve his own lot must rely on his own strength and effort. The vote of the consumers passes judgment without respect to persons. The achievements of the candidate, not his person, are valued. Work well done and services well rendered are the only means to succeed.

Under socialism, on the contrary, the beginner must please those already settled. They do not like too efficient newcomers. (Neither do old-established entrepreneurs like such men; but, under the supremacy of the consumers, they cannot prevent their competition.) In the bureaucratic machine of socialism the way toward promotion is not achievement but the favor of the superiors. The youth depends entirely on the kind disposition of the old men. The rising generation is at the mercy of the aged.

It is useless to deny this fact. There are no Marxian classes within a socialist society. But there is an irreconcilable conflict between those who are in favor with Stalin and Hitler and those who are not. And it is simply human for a dictator to prefer those who share his opinions and praise his work to those who do not.

It was in vain that the Italian Fascists made a hymn to youth their party song and that the Austrian socialists taught the children to sing: "We are young and this is fine." It is not fine to be a young man under bureaucratic management. The only right that young people enjoy under this system is to be docile, submissive, and obedient. There is no room for unruly innovators who have their own ideas.

This is more than a crisis of the youth. It is a crisis of

progress and civilization. Mankind is doomed when the youths are deprived of the opportunity to remodel society according to their own fashion.

3. AUTHORITARIAN GUARDIANSHIP AND PROGRESS

Paternal government by an order of lofty and wise men, by any elite of noble bureaucrats, can claim a very eminent champion, Plato.

Plato's ideal and perfect state is to be ruled by unselfish philosophers. They are unbribable judges and impartial administrators, strictly abiding by the eternal immutable laws of justice. For this is the characteristic mark of Plato's philosophy: it does not pay any attention to the evolution of social and economic conditions and to changes in human ideas concerning ends and means. There exists the perennial pattern of the good state, and every deviation of actual conditions from this model cannot be anything else than corruption and degradation. The problem is simply to establish the perfect society and then to keep it from any alteration, as change must be tantamount to deterioration. Social and economic institutions are rigid. The notion of progress in knowledge, in technological procedures, in business methods, and in social organization is foreign to Plato's mind. And all later utopians who shaped the blueprints of their earthly paradises according to Plato's example in the same way believed in the immutability of human affairs.

Plato's ideal of elite rule has been converted into fact by the Catholic Church. The Roman Church, under the Tridentine organization as it emerged from the Counter-Reformation, is a perfect bureaucracy. It has successfully solved the most delicate problem of every nondemocratic government, the selection of the top executives. To every boy access to the highest dignities of the Church is virtually open. The local priest is anxious to smooth the way to education for the most intelligent youths of his parish; they are trained in the Bishop's seminary; once ordained, their further career depends entirely upon their character, their zeal, and their intellect. There are among the prelates many scions of noble and wealthy families. But they do not owe their office to their ancestry. They have to compete, on almost equal terms, with the sons of poor peasants, workers, and serfs. The princes of the Catholic Church, the abbots and the teachers of the theological universities, are a body of eminent men. Even in the most advanced countries they are worthy rivals of the most brilliant scholars, philosophers, scientists, and statesmen.

It is to this marvelous instance that the authors of all modern socialist utopias refer as an example. The case is manifest with two forerunners of present-day socialism: Count Henri de Saint-Simon and Auguste Comte. But it was essentially the same with most other socialist authors, although for obvious reasons they did not point to the Church as a model. No precedent of a perfect hierarchy could be found other than that presented by Catholicism.

However, the reference to the Church is fallacious. The realm of Christianity which the Pope and the other Bishops administer is not subject to any change. It is built upon a perennial and immutable doctrine. The creed is fixed forever. There is no progress and no evolution. There is only obedience to the law and the dogma. The methods of selection adopted by the Church are very efficient in the government of a body clinging to an undisputed, unchangeable set of rules and regulations. They are perfect in the choice of the guardians of an eternal treasure of doctrine.

But the case of human society and civil government is different. It is the most precious privilege of man to strive ceaselessly for improvement and to fight by improved methods against the obstacles that nature opposes to his life and welfare. This innate impulse has transformed the descendants of crude cave dwellers into the somewhat civilized men of our age. But mankind has not yet reached a state of perfection beyond which no further progress is possible. The forces that brought about our present civilization are not dead. If not tied by a rigid system of social organization, they will go on and bring further improvement. The selective principle according to which the Catholic Church chooses its future chiefs is unswerving devotion to the creed and its dogmas. It does not look for innovators and reformers, for pioneers of new ideas radically opposed to the old ones. This is what the appointment of the future top executives by the old and well-tried present rulers can safeguard. No bureaucratic system can achieve anything else. But it is precisely this adamant conservatism that makes bureaucratic methods utterly inadequate for the conduct of social and economic affairs.

Bureaucratization is necessarily rigid because it involves the observation of established rules and practices. But in social life rigidity amounts to petrification and death. It is a very significant fact that stability and security are the most cherished slogans of present-day "reformers." If primitive men had adopted the principle of stability, they would never have gained security; they would long since have been wiped out by beasts of prey and microbes.

German Marxians coined the dictum: If socialism is against human nature, then human nature must be changed. They did not realize that if man's nature is changed, he ceases to be a man. In an all-round bureaucratic system neither the bureaucrats nor their subjects would any longer be real human beings.

4. THE SELECTION OF THE DICTATOR

All champions of salvation through the rule of noble despots blithely assume that there cannot be any doubt about the question of who this lofty ruler or class of rulers should be and that all men will voluntarily yield to the supremacy of this superhuman dictator or aristocracy. They do not realize that many men and groups of men could claim primacy for themselves. If the decision between various candidates is not left to majority vote, no principle of selection remains other than civil war. The alternative to the democratic principle of selection through popular election is the seizure of power by ruthless adventurers.

In the second century after Christ the Roman Empire was ruled according to a sublime elaboration of the Führer principle. The Emperor was the most able and eminent man. He did not bequeath his dignity to a member of his family, but he chose as successor the man whom he considered best fitted for the office. This system gave the Empire a succession of four great monarchs: Trajan, Hadrian, Antoninus Pius, and Marcus Aurelius. But then followed the era of the Praetorians, continuous civil war, anarchy, and rapid decay. The rule of the worst was substituted for the rule of the best. Ambitious generals, supported by mercenaries, seized power and ruled until another adventurer defeated them. Treachery, rebellion, and murder became the selective principle. Historians blame Marcus Aurelius, the last of the good emperors. He was guilty, they say, because he abandoned the practice of his predecessors and, instead of choosing the most suitable man, installed his incompetent son Commodus. However, a system that can be wrecked by the fault of only one man is a bad system, even if the fault were less pardonable and understandable than that of a father overrating the character and capacity of his offspring. The truth is that such a Führer system must necessarily result in permanent civil war as soon as there are several candidates for the supreme office.

All present-day dictators came into office through violence. They later had to defend their supremacy against the aspirations of rivals. Political language has coined a special term to refer to such actions: they are called *purges*. The successors of these dictators will rise to power through the same methods and will apply the same cruelty and ruthlessness in maintaining it. The ultimate basis of an all-round bureaucratic system is violence. The security that it allegedly gives is the turmoil of endless civil war.

5. THE VANISHING OF THE CRITICAL SENSE

The socialists assert that capitalism is degrading, that it is incompatible with man's dignity, that it weakens man's intellectual abilities and spoils his moral integrity. Under capitalism, they say, everybody must regard his fellow men as competitors. Man's innate instincts of benevolence and companionship are thus converted into hatred and a ruthless striving for personal success at the expense of all other people. But socialism will restore the virtues of human nature. Amicableness, fraternity, and comradeship will be the characteristic features of future man. What is needed first is to eliminate this worst of all evils, competition.

However, competition can never be eliminated. As there will always be positions which men value more highly than other positions, people will strive for them and try to outstrip their rivals. It is immaterial whether we call this emulation rivalry or competition. At any rate, in some way or other it must be decided whether or not a man ought to get the job he is applying for. The question is only what kind of competition should exist.

The capitalist variety of competition is to outdo other people on the market through offering better and cheaper goods. The bureaucratic variety consists in intrigues at the "courts" of those in power.

There was a good deal of flattery, adulation, servility, and cringing at the courts of all despotic rulers. But there had always been some men at least who were not afraid to tell a tyrant the truth. It is different in our day. Politicians and writers outdo one another in the adulation of the sovereign, the "common man." They do not venture to impair their popularity by the expression of unpopular ideas. The courtiers of Louis XIV never went as far as some people go today in praising the Führers and their supporters, the masses. It seems that our contemporaries have lost all common sense and self-criticism.

At a Communist Party Congress a writer named Avd-yenko addressed Stalin in these terms: "Centuries shall elapse and the communist generations of the future will deem us the happiest of all mortals that have inhabited this planet throughout the ages, because we have seen Stalin the leader genius, Stalin the Sage, the smiling, the kindly, the supremely simple. When I met Stalin, even at a distance, I throbbed with his forcefulness, his magnetism, and his greatness. I wanted to sing, to shriek, to howl from happiness and exaltation." [1] A bureaucrat addressing his superior on whom his promotion depends is less poetic but no less crawling.

When at the Diamond Jubilee of Emperor Francis Joseph a statistician attributed to the Emperor's credit that after sixty years of his reign the country had many thousands of miles of railroads, while at its beginning there were much fewer, the public (and probably the Emperor himself) simply laughed at this piece of toadyism. But nobody laughed when the Soviet Government in the World's Fairs of Paris and New York flamboyantly boasted of the fact that while the Russia of the Czars used no tractors at all, a quarter of a century later it had already imitated this new American invention.

Nobody ever believed that the paternal absolutism of Marie Thérèse and her grandson Francis was justified by the fact that Mozart, Haydn, Beethoven, and Schubert composed immortal music. But the symphony of a contemporary Russian composer who probably will be forgotten after a few years is claimed as a proof of the eminence of Soviet totalitarianism.

The question is whether the system of bureaucratic control or the system of economic freedom is more efficient. This question can be answered only by economic reasoning. The mere assertion of the fact that the cigarettes manufactured by the French Government's tobacco monopoly were

1. As quoted by W. H. Chamberlin, *Collectivism, a False Utopia* (New York, 1937), p. 43.

not so bad as to induce the French to give up smoking is not an argument in favor of government operation of industry. Neither is the fact that the cigarettes manufactured by the Greek Government's monopoly were the delight of smokers. It is not a merit of the Greek bureaucrats that the climatic and physical conditions of their country make the tobacco grown by the peasants delicate and fragrant.

Every German took it for granted that the very essence and nature of things make it imperative that universities, railroads, telegraphs, and telephones be operated by the government. For a Russian the idea that a man could live without a passport, duly issued and authenticated by the police, always seemed paradoxical. Under the conditions that developed in the last thirty years the citizens of continental Europe became mere appurtenances of their identification papers. In many countries it was risky to go out for a walk without these documents. In most European countries a man has not been free to stay overnight in any place without immediately reporting to the local police department his sleeping place and every change of address.[2]

It is possible that some good may be derived from such regimentation. Of course, it is not of much use in fighting crime and prosecuting criminals. A murderer in hiding will not shrink from violating the law requiring a report of any change of address.[3] In defending their system the bureaucrats become melodramatic. They ask the public how poor abandoned children could find their unscrupulous parents again. They do not mention that a smart detective might be able to find them. Moreover, the fact that there

2. Thus the files of the police departments of many European cities provide full information for the last hundred or even hundred and fifty years concerning every resident's or visitor's sojourn and all his changes of address. A priceless and well-exploited source of knowledge indeed for biographers.

3. It seems curious to Americans that in many European trials the jury was asked to answer two questions like this: First, is the defendant guilty of having murdered the victim? Secondly, is the defendant guilty of not having duly reported his change of address?

are some scoundrels cannot be considered a sufficient reason for restricting the freedom of the immense majority of decent people.

A profit-seeking enterprise is supported by the voluntary patronage of the public. It cannot subsist if customers do not pour in. But the bureaus forcibly acquire their "patrons." That an office is approached by many people is not proof of its satisfying an urgent need of the people. It only shows that it interferes with matters that are important to the life of everyone.

The fading of the critical sense is a serious menace to the preservation of our civilization. It makes it easy for quacks to fool the people. It is remarkable that the educated strata are more gullible than the less educated. The most enthusiastic supporters of Marxism, Nazism, and Fascism were the intellectuals, not the boors. The intellectuals were never keen enough to see the manifest contradictions of their creeds. It did not in the least impair the popularity of Fascism that Mussolini in the same speech praised the Italians as the representatives of the oldest Western civilization and as the youngest among the civilized nations. No German nationalist minded it when dark-haired Hitler, corpulent Goering, and lame Goebbels were praised as the shining representatives of the tall, slim, fair-haired, heroic Aryan master race. Is it not amazing that many millions of non-Russians are firmly convinced that the Soviet regime is democratic, even more democratic than America?

This absence of criticism makes it possible to tell people that they will be free men in a system of all-round regimentation. People imagine a regime in which all means are owned by the state and the government is the sole employer as a realm of freedom. They never take into account the possibility that the almighty government of their utopia could aim at ends of which they themselves entirely disapprove. They always tacitly assume that the dictator will do exactly what they themselves want him to do.

VII

IS THERE ANY REMEDY
AVAILABLE?

I. PAST FAILURES

WE must acknowledge the fact that hitherto all endeavors to stop the further advance of bureaucratization and socialization have been in vain. In the twenty-seven years that have passed since President Wilson led America into the war to make the world safe for democracy, democracy has lost more and more ground. Despotism triumphs in most of the European countries. Even America has adopted policies which, some decades ago, it disparaged as "Prussian." Mankind is manifestly moving toward totalitarianism. The rising generation yearns for full government control of every sphere of life.

Learned lawyers have published excellent treatises depicting the progressive substitution of administrative arbitrariness for the rule of law.[1] They have told the story of how the undermining of self-government makes all the rights of the individual citizen disappear and results in a hyperdespotism of the oriental style. But the socialists do not care a whit for freedom and private initiative.

Neither have satirical books been more successful than the ponderous tomes of the lawyers. Some of the most eminent writers of the nineteenth century—Balzac, Dickens, Gogol, Maupassant, Courteline—have struck devastating

---

1. It may suffice to quote two of the most brilliant books of this class: *The New Despotism* by Lord Hewart of Bury, Lord Chief Justice of England (New York, 1929), and *Our Wonderland of Bureaucracy* by James M. Beck, former Solicitor General of the United States (New York, 1932). It is noteworthy that the latter book was published before the inauguration of the New Deal.

blows against bureaucratism. Aldous Huxley was even courageous enough to make socialism's dreamed paradise the target of his sardonic irony. The public was delighted. But his readers rushed nonetheless to apply for jobs with the government.

Some people like to make fun of especially extravagant features of bureaucracy. It is indeed curious that the government of the world's most powerful and richest nation runs an office—the Bureau of Home Economics of the United States Department of Agriculture—one of the tasks of which is to design trousers "for the very small child who is just learning to dress himself." But for many of our contemporaries there is nothing ridiculous in this. They aim at a mode of government under which the production of hose, underwear, and all other useful things should be a task of the authorities.

All learned criticisms and witty satires are of no avail because they do not hit the core of the problem. Bureaucratization is only a particular feature of socialization. The main matter is: Capitalism or Socialism? Which?

The supporters of socialism contend that capitalism is an unfair system of exploitation, that it is extremely detrimental to the welfare of the masses and that it results in misery, degradation, and progressive pauperization of the immense majority. On the other hand, they depict their socialist utopia as a promised land of milk and honey in which everybody will be happy and rich. Are they right or are they wrong? This is the question.

2. ECONOMICS VERSUS PLANNING AND TOTALITARIANISM

This is entirely an economic problem. It cannot be decided without entering into a full scrutiny of economics. The spurious catchwords and fallacious doctrines of the advocates of government control, socialism, communism, planning, and totalitarianism cannot be unmasked except by economic reasoning. Whether one likes it or not, it is a fact that the main issues of present-day politics are purely economic and cannot be understood without a grasp of economic theory. Only a man conversant with the main problems of economics is in a position to form an independent opinion on the problems involved. All the others are merely repeating what they have picked up by the way. They are an easy prey to demagogic swindlers and idiotic quacks. Their gullibility is the most serious menace to the preservation of democracy and to Western civilization.

The first duty of a citizen of a democratic community is to educate himself and to acquire the knowledge needed for dealing with civic affairs. The franchise is not a privilege but a duty and a moral responsibility. The voter is virtually an officeholder; his office is the supreme one and implies the highest obligation. A citizen fully absorbed by his scientific work in other fields or by his calling as an artist may plead extenuating circumstances when failing in this task of self-instruction. Perhaps such men are right in pretending that they have more important tasks to fulfill. But all the other *intelligent* men are not only frivolous but mischievous in neglecting to educate and instruct themselves for the best performance of their duties as sovereign voters.

The main propaganda trick of the supporters of the allegedly "progressive" policy of government control is to blame capitalism for all that is unsatisfactory in present-day conditions and to extol the blessings which socialism has in store for mankind. They have never attempted to prove their fallacious dogmas or still less to refute the objections raised by the economists. All they did was to call their adversaries names and to cast suspicion upon their motives. And, unfortunately, the average citizen cannot see through these stratagems.

Consider, for instance, the problem of mass unemployment prolonged year after year. The "progressive" interprets it as an evil inherent in capitalism. The naïve public is ready to swallow this explanation. People do not realize that in an unhampered labor market, manipulated neither by labor-union pressure nor by government-fixed minimum wage rates, unemployment affects only small groups for a short time. Under free capitalism unemployment is a comparatively unimportant temporary phenomenon; there prevails a permanent tendency for unemployment to disappear. Economic changes may bring about new unemployment. But at the wage rates established in a free labor market everyone eager to earn wages finally gets a job. Unemployment as a mass phenomenon is the outcome of allegedly "pro-labor" policies of the governments and of labor-union pressure and compulsion.

This explanation is by no means peculiar to those economists whom the "progressives" call "reactionaries." Karl Marx himself was fully convinced that labor unions cannot succeed in raising wage rates for all workers. The Marxian doctrinaires for many years firmly opposed all endeavors to fix minimum wage rates. They deemed such measures contrary to the interests of the great majority of wage earners.

It is an illusion to believe that government spending can create jobs for the unemployed, that is, for those who cannot get jobs on account of the labor unions' or the government's policies. If the government's spending is financed by noninflationary methods, that is, either by taxing the citizens or by borrowing from the public, it abolishes on the one hand as many jobs as it creates on the other. If it is financed by inflation, that is, either by an increase of money and bank notes in circulation or by borrowing from the commercial banks, it reduces unemployment only if money wages lag behind the rise of commodity prices, that is, if and so far as *real* wage rates drop. There is but one way toward an increase of real wage rates for all those eager to earn wages: the progressive accumulation of new capital and the improvement of technical methods of production which the new capital brings about. The true interests of labor coincide with those of business.

The approach to a grasp of economic problems does not consist in an indiscriminate assimilation of more or less disconnected facts and figures. It consists rather in a careful analysis and examination of conditions by reasonable reflection. What is needed above all is *common sense* and logical clarity. Go right to the bottom of things is the main rule. Do not acquiesce in superficial explanations and solutions. Use your power of thinking and your critical abilities.

It would be a serious blunder to believe that this recommendation of economic studies aims at a substitution of another brand of propaganda for the propaganda of the various governments and parties. Propaganda is one of the worst evils of bureaucracy and socialism. Propaganda is always the propaganda of lies, fallacies, and superstitions. *Truth does not need any propaganda;* it holds its own. The characteristic mark of truth is that it is the correct representation of reality, i.e., of a state of affairs that is and works whether or not anybody recognizes it. The recognition and pronouncement of truth is as such a condemnation of everything that is untrue. It carries on by the mere fact of being true.

Therefore let the false prophets go on. Do not try to imitate their policies. Do not try as they do to silence and to outlaw dissenters. The liars must be afraid of truth and are therefore driven to suppress its pronouncement. But the advocates of truth put their hopes upon their own rightness. Veracity does not fear the liars. It can stand their competition. The propagandists may continue to spread their fables and to indoctrinate youth. They will fail lamentably.

Lenin and Hitler knew very well why they abolished freedom of thought, speech, and the press, and why they closed the frontiers of their countries to any import of ideas from abroad. Their systems could not survive without concentration camps, censors, and hangmen. Their main instruments are the G.P.U. and the Gestapo.

The British champions of socialization and bureaucratization are no less fully aware than the Bolsheviks and the Nazis of the fact that under freedom of speech and thought they will never achieve their ends. Professor Harold Laski is frank enough to declare that a restriction of Parliament's powers is necessary to safeguard the transition to socialism.[2] Sir Stafford Cripps, the favorite candidate of the self-styled liberals for Prime Minister, has advised a "Planning and Enabling Act" which, once passed by Parliament, could not be discussed, still less repealed again. By virtue of this act, which should be very general and leave all "details" to the Cabinet, the Government would be endowed with irrevocable powers. Its orders and decrees should never be considered by Parliament; neither should there be a recourse to the Courts of Justice. All offices should be manned by "staunch party members," by "persons of known Socialist views."[3] The British "Council of Clergy and Ministers for Common Ownership" declares in a pamphlet to which the Bishop of Bradford wrote the foreword that the establishment of real and permanent socialism requires "that all the fundamental opposition must be liquidated, i.e., rendered politically inactive by disfranchisement, and, if necessary, by imprisonment."[4] Professor Joan Robinson of Cambridge University, second only to Lord Keynes himself in the leadership of the Keynesian school, is no less intolerant in her zeal to realize socialism. In her opinion "the notion of freedom is a slippery one." It is "only when there is no serious enemy, without or within, that full freedom of speech can be safely allowed." Mrs. Robinson is not only afraid of independent churches, universities, learned societies, and publishing houses, but no less of independent theaters and philharmonic societies. All such institutions, she contends, should be allowed to exist only "provided the

2. Laski, *Democracy in Crisis* (London, 1933), p. 87. For a masterful refutation of Laski's antidemocratic ideas cf. Rappard, *The Crisis of Democracy* (Chicago, 1938), pp. 213–216.

3. Cf. the brilliant article of James Truslow Adams, "Planners See Where Planning Leads" in *Barron's National Business and Financial Weekly* of January 31, 1944, p. 3.

4. Ibid.

regime is sufficiently secure to risk criticism." [5] And another distinguished advocate of British collectivism, J. G. Crowther, does not shrink from praising the blessings of inquisition.[6] What a pity the Stuarts did not live to witness the triumph of their principles!

Thus the most eminent advocates of socialism implicitly admit that their tenets and plans cannot stand the criticism of economic science and are doomed under a regime of freedom.

But as happily there are still some free countries left there is still some hope for a resurrection of truth.

3. THE PLAIN CITIZEN VERSUS THE PROFESSIONAL PROPAGANDIST OF BUREAUCRATIZATION

The aim of the popularization of economic studies is not to make every man an economist. The idea is to equip the citizen for his civic functions in community life.

The conflict between capitalism and totalitarianism, on the outcome of which the fate of civilization depends, will not be decided by civil wars and revolutions. It is a war of ideas. Public opinion will determine victory and defeat.

Wherever and whenever men meet for discussing any affairs of their municipality, state, or nation, public opinion is in the process of evolving and changing, however trifling the immediate topic concerned may be. Public opinion is influenced by anything that is spoken or done in transactions between buyers and sellers, between employers and employees, between creditors and debtors. Public opinion is

5. Joan Robinson, *Private Enterprise or Public Control* (Handbooks for Discussion Groups, published for the Association for Education in Citizenship by the English Universities Press Ltd.), pp. 13–14. It is strange that in the Preface to this booklet the Association declares "we advocate democracy" and points out that its objective is to train the citizens "in respect for the equal rights and freedoms of others."

6. J. G. Crowther, *Social Relations of Science* (Macmillan, 1941), pp. 331, 333.

shaped in the debates of countless representative bodies, committees and commissions, associations and clubs, by editorials and letters to the editor, by the pleading of lawyers and by the opinions of judges.

In all these discussions the professionals have an advantage over the laymen. The odds are always in favor of those who devote all their effort exclusively to one thing only. Although not necessarily experts and often certainly not more clever than the amateurs, they enjoy the benefit of being specialists. Their eristic technique as well as their training are superior. They come to the encounter with rested mind and body, not tired after a long day's work like the amateurs.

Now, almost all these professionals are zealous advocates of bureaucratism and socialism. There are, first of all, the hosts of employees of the governments' and the various parties' propaganda offices. There are furthermore the teachers of various educational institutions which curiously enough consider the avowal of bureaucratic, socialist, or Marxian radicalism the mark of scientific perfection. There are the editors and contributors of "progressive" newspapers and magazines, labor-union leaders and organizers, and finally leisured ambitious men anxious to get into the headlines by the expression of radical views. The ordinary businessman, lawyer, or wage earner is no match for them.

The layman may brilliantly succeed in proving his argument. It is of no use. For his adversary, clothed with the full dignity of his office or his professorship, shouts back: "The fallacy of the gentleman's reasoning has long since been unmasked by the famous German professors, Mayer, Müller, and Schmid. Only an idiot can still cling to such antiquated and done-for ideas." The layman is discredited in the eyes of the audience, fully trusting in professional infallibility. He does not know how to answer. He has never heard the names of these eminent German professors. Thus he does not know that their books are simple humbug, full of nonsense, and that they did not touch the problems

which he raised. He may learn it later. But that cannot alter
the fact that he has been defeated on the spot.

Or the layman may cleverly demonstrate the impracticability of some project suggested. Then the professional re-
torts: "This gentleman is so ignorant as not to know that
the scheme proposed succeeded very well in socialist
Sweden and in *red* Vienna." Again our layman is silenced.
How can he know that almost all English-language books
on Sweden and Vienna are propaganda products badly dis-
torting the facts? He has not had the opportunity of getting
correct information from the original sources.

The climax of the professional's oratory is, of course, always the reference to Russia, the paradise of the workers
and peasants. For almost thirty years only fanatical com-
munists and fellow travelers were permitted to enter Russia. Their reports are uncritical glorifications of the Soviets,
some of them utterly dishonest, the rest childish in their
naïve credulity. It is one of the most comforting facts that
some of these travelers abandoned in Russia their pro-
Soviet leanings and, back home, published unvarnished
accounts. But the professionals easily dispose of these books
by calling their authors "Fascists."

What is needed is to make the civic leaders fit for such
encounters with professional preachers of bureaucratization
and socialization. It is hopeless to stop the trend toward
bureaucratization by the mere expression of indignation and
by a nostalgic glorification of the good old times. These old
days were not so good as they appear to some of our contemporaries. What was great in them was their reliance on
the tendency toward improvement inherent in the system
of unhampered market economy. They did not believe in
the government's godlikeness. This was their glory.

The most detrimental outcome of the average citizen's
repugnance to a serious concern with economic problems is
his readiness to back a program of compromise. He looks
upon the conflict between capitalism and socialism as if it
were a quarrel between two groups—labor and capital—

each of which claims for itself the whole of the matter at issue. As he himself is not prepared to appraise the merits of the arguments advanced by each of the parties, he thinks it would be a fair solution to end the dispute by an amicable arrangement: each claimant should have a part of his claim. Thus the program of government interference with business acquired its prestige. There should be neither full capitalism nor full socialism, but something in between, a middle way. This third system, assert its supporters, should be capitalism regulated and regimented by government interference with business. But this government intervention should not amount to full government control of all economic activities; it should be limited to the elimination of some especially objectionable excrescences of capitalism without suppressing the activities of the entrepreneur altogether. Thus a social order will result which is allegedly as far from full capitalism as it is from pure socialism, and while retaining the advantages inherent in each of these two systems will avoid their disadvantages. Almost all those who do not unconditionally advocate full socialism support this system of interventionism today and all governments which are not outright and frankly pro-socialist have espoused a policy of economic interventionism. There are nowadays very few who oppose any kind of government interference with prices, wage rates, interest rates, and profits and are not afraid to contend that they consider capitalism and free enterprise the only workable system, beneficial to the whole of society and to all its members.

Yet, the reasoning of the advocates of this middle solution is entirely fallacious. The conflict between socialism and capitalism is not a struggle between two parties for a greater share in the social dividend. To see the matter this way is tantamount to a full acceptance of the tenets of the Marxians and the other socialists. The adversaries of socialism deny that any class or group would fare better under socialism than under outright capitalism. They contest the thesis that the workers would be better off in a socialist commonwealth and are, consequently, wronged by the very existence of the capitalist system. *They do not recommend capitalism for the sake of selfish interests of the entrepreneurs and capitalists but for the sake of all members of society.* The great historical conflict concerning the problem of society's economic organization cannot be dealt with like a quarrel between two businessmen concerning an amount of money; it cannot be solved by splitting the difference.

Economic interventionism is a self-defeating policy. The individual measures that it applies do not achieve the results sought. They bring about a state of affairs, which—from the viewpoint of its advocates themselves—is much more undesirable than the previous state they intended to alter. Unemployment of a great part of those ready to earn wages, prolonged year after year, monopoly, economic crisis, general restriction of the productivity of economic effort, economic nationalism, and war are the inescapable consequences of government interference with business as recommended by the supporters of the third solution. All those evils for which the socialists blame capitalism are precisely the product of this unfortunate, allegedly "progressive" policy. The catastrophic events which are grist for the mills of the radical socialists are the outcome of the ideas of those who say: "I am not against capitalism, but . . ." Such people are virtually nothing but pacemakers of socialization and thorough bureaucratization. Their ignorance begets disaster.

Division of labor and specialization are essential features of civilization. But for them both material prosperity and intellectual progress would be impossible. The existence of an integrated group of scientists, scholars, and research workers is an outcome of the division of labor just as is the existence of any other class of specialists. The man who specializes in economics is a specialist like all other specialists. The further advancement of economic science will in the future also be an achievement of men devoting all their endeavors to this task.

But it would be a fateful error for the citizens to leave concern with economic studies to the professionals as their exclusive domain. As the main issues of present-day politics are essentially economic, such a resignation would amount to a complete abdication of the citizens for the benefit of the professionals. If the voters or the members of a parliament are faced with the problems raised by a bill concerning the prevention of cattle diseases or the construction of an office building, they may leave the discussion of the details to the experts. Such veterinarian and engineering problems do not interfere with the fundamentals of social and political life. They are important but not primary and vital. But if not only the masses but even the greater part of their elected representatives declare: "These monetary problems can only be comprehended by specialists; we do not have the inclination to study them; in this matter we must trust the experts," they are virtually renouncing their sovereignty to the professionals. It does not matter whether or not they formally delegate their powers to legislate or not. At any rate the specialists outstrip them. The bureaucrats carry on.

The plain citizens are mistaken in complaining that the bureaucrats have arrogated powers; they themselves and their mandatories have abandoned their sovereignty. Their ignorance of fundamental problems of economics has made the professional specialists supreme. All technical and juridical details of legislation can and must be left to the experts. But democracy becomes impracticable if the eminent citizens, the intellectual leaders of the community, are not in a position to form their own opinion on the basic social, economic, and political principles of policies. If the citizens are under the intellectual hegemony of the bureaucratic professionals, society breaks up into two castes: the ruling professionals, the Brahmins, and the gullible citizenry. Then despotism emerges, whatever the wording of constitutions and laws may be.

Democracy means self-determination. How can people

determine their own affairs if they are too indifferent to gain through their own thinking an independent judgment on fundamental political and economic problems? Democracy is not a good that people can enjoy without trouble. It is, on the contrary, a treasure that must be daily defended and conquered anew by strenuous effort.

CONCLUSION

THE analysis of the technical characteristics of bureaucratic management and of its opposite, profit management, provides a clue for a fair and unbiased valuation of both systems of doing things under the division of labor.

Public administration, the handling of the government apparatus of coercion and compulsion, must necessarily be formalistic and bureaucratic. No reform can remove the bureaucratic features of the government's bureaus. It is useless to blame them for their slowness and slackness. It is vain to lament over the fact that the assiduity, carefulness, and painstaking work of the average bureau clerk are, as a rule, below those of the average worker in private business. (There are, after all, many civil servants whose enthusiastic fervor amounts to unselfish sacrifice.) In the absence of an unquestionable yardstick of success and failure it is almost impossible for the vast majority of men to find that incentive to utmost exertion that the money calculus of profit-seeking business easily provides. It is of no use to criticize the bureaucrat's pedantic observance of rigid rules and regulations. Such rules are indispensable if public administration is not to slip out of the hands of the top executives and degenerate into the supremacy of subordinate clerks. These rules are, moreover, the only means of making the law supreme in the conduct of public affairs and of protecting the citizen against despotic arbitrariness.

It is easy for an observer to indict the bureaucratic apparatus for extravagance. But the executive with whom the responsibility for perfect service rests sees the matter from another angle. He does not want to run too high a risk. He prefers to be on the safe side and to be doubly sure.

All such deficiencies are inherent in the performance of services which cannot be checked by money statements of profit and loss. Indeed we would never have recognized that they really are deficiencies if we were not in a position to compare the bureaucratic system with the operation of profit-seeking enterprise. This much-abused system of the "mean" striving for profit made people efficiency conscious and eager for the utmost rationalization. But we cannot help it. We must put up with the fact that one cannot apply to a police department or to the office of a tax collector the well-tried methods of profit-seeking business.

Yet the whole matter takes on a quite different meaning in view of the fanatical endeavors to transform the entire apparatus of production and distribution into a mammoth bureau. Lenin's ideal of taking the organization of the government's postal service as the pattern of society's economic organization and of making every man a cog in a vast bureaucratic machine [1] makes it imperative to unmask the inferiority of bureaucratic methods when compared with those of private business. The aim of such a scrutiny is certainly not to disparage the work of tax collectors, customs officers, and patrolmen or to belittle their achievements. But it is necessary to show in what essential respects a steel plant differs from an embassy and a shoe plant from a marriage license bureau, and why it would be mischievous to reorganize a bakery according to the pattern of the post office.

What is called in a very biased terminology the substitution of the service principle for the profit principle would result in an abandonment of the only method making for rationality and calculation in the production of necessities. The profit earned by the entrepreneur is expressive of the fact that he has well served the consumers, that is, all the people. But with regard to the performance of bureaus no method for establishing success or failure by calculation procedures is available.

In any socialist system the central board of production management alone would have the power to order, and

1. Lenin, *State and Revolution* (1917; New York ed., 1935), p. 44.

everybody else would have to carry out the orders received. All people except the production czar would have to comply unconditionally with instructions, codes, rules, and regulations drafted by a superior body. Of course every citizen might have the right to suggest some changes in this immense system of regimentation. But the way from such a suggestion to its acceptance by the competent supreme authority would at best be as far and onerous as the way is today from a letter to the editor or an article in a periodical suggesting an amendment of a law to its passage by the legislature.

There have been in the course of history many movements asking with enthusiasm and fanaticism for a reform of social institutions. People fought for their religious convictions, for the preservation of their civilization, for freedom, for self-determination, for the abolition of serfdom and slavery, for fairness and justice in court procedure. Today millions are fascinated by the plan to transform the whole world into a bureau, to make everybody a bureaucrat, and to wipe out any private initiative. The paradise of the future is visualized as an all-embracing bureaucratic apparatus. The most powerful reform movement that history has ever known, the first ideological trend not limited to a section of mankind only but supported by people of all races, nations, religions, and civilizations aims at all-round bureaucratization. The post office is the model for the construction of the New Jerusalem. The post-office clerk is the prototype of future man. Streams of blood have been shed for the realization of this ideal.

In this book we are discussing not persons but systems of social organization. We do not mean that the post-office clerk is inferior to anybody else. What must be realized is only that the strait jacket of bureaucratic organization paralyzes the individual's initiative, while within the capitalist market society an innovator still has a chance to succeed. The former makes for stagnation and preservation of inveterate methods, the latter makes for progress and improvement. Capitalism is progressive, socialism is not. One does not invalidate this argument by pointing out that the Bolshevists have copied various American innovations. So did all oriental peoples. But it is a non sequitur to deduce from this fact that all civilized nations must copy the Russian methods of social organization.

The champions of socialism call themselves progressives, but they recommend a system which is characterized by rigid observance of routine and by a resistance to every kind of improvement. They call themselves liberals, but they are intent upon abolishing liberty. They call themselves democrats, but they yearn for dictatorship. They call themselves revolutionaries, but they want to make the government omnipotent. They promise the blessings of the Garden of Eden, but they plan to transform the world into a gigantic post office. Every man but one a subordinate clerk in a bureau, what an alluring utopia! What a noble cause to fight for!

Against all this frenzy of agitation there is but one weapon available: reason. Just common sense is needed to prevent man from falling prey to illusory fantasies and empty catchwords.